Hungers of the Human Heart

by Dr.Kermit L. Long

This book is reprinted by permission.
Friendship Press
Phoenix, AZ

Library of Congress Catalog Card Number: 64-10440

ISBN 1-893482-01-4

Printed by:
Images Plus
Madison, WI, USA

CONTENTS

DEDICATED TO THE SEEKERS FOR

MEANING
LOVE
LIFE
PEACE
JOY
FULFILLMENT
GOD

INTRODUCTION

I shrink whenever a book comes along with some such title as "A Message to Intellectuals" or "A Word to Women" or "Sermons to Conservatives." I because the gospel is universal, and whenever we assume it ought to be directed to one class, one sex, one age, we betray our misunderstanding of it. Indeed this excessive division of life into special interest groups is one of the diseases of our time.

You can imagine, therefore, with what enthusiasm I approached a book with the title: Hungers of the Human Heart. Here is the human situation and, when a man aims at this target, his preaching has the right direction and the right goal.

The writer is a preacher and a pastor. He is one of my fine friends and has won my admiration for his outstanding work. His writing does not rise out of theory but out of practice. His preaching has the warmth and concern which attracts people of all sorts and conditions.

So I take great delight in being allowed to introduce this book. I think it will help all persons, both lay and ministerial. There is a quality of excitement in it which is the mark of good preaching.
— Gerald Kennedy

Preface

Life was not meant to be dull and uninteresting. It ought to be filled with the excitement of eternal joy. God never intended for us to allow our days to be cluttered with the inconsequential or filled with nothingness, Never did the Creator mean that we should settle for average mediocrity. He has put deep within us the desires for greatness — the natural hungers of our hearts — for we were made to reflect his glory as revealed in Christ Jesus our Lord. Dedication to the Master of life in daily discipleship will satisfy these hungers and help us live as God intended.

It is to this theme that my book is directed. The following chapters represent lectures delivered in pastors' schools, annual conferences, the Dennison Lectures and sermons preached in spiritual life missions, evangelistic rallies, and from a number of pulpits in America and abroad. It is my prayer that you the reader, will be blest as a result of my efforts.

It is impossible to adequately express my thanks to all who have helped make this book a reality. I ever continue to he humbled by my debt of gratitude to the many laymen of the churches I have been privileged to serve. They are among God's finest. They bless and inspire this preacher. Without their encouragement and insistence this book would probably not yet be written.

I wish you, my fellow seeker, the joy of discovery.

— Kermit L. Long

Hungers
of the
Human
Heart

Chapter One
Hungers of the Human Heart

"I am the bread of life." - John 6:35

A psychology professor would speak of the psychological desires of mankind. He might also refer to the inner urges of people. But I, as a preacher, have decided to call these desires and urges the hungers of the human heart. These hungers are basically spiritual in nature. Therefore they will never be satisfied until they are met with spiritual food.

In the sixth chapter of the Gospel According to John, we find the multitudes clamoring for Jesus. They wanted some sign, some miracle, forgetting that Jesus was and is the greatest of all miracles. They told the Master that their ancestors had eaten manna in the desert. Jesus then told them that it was the Father, not Moses, who provided the bread. Jesus admonished them not to be content to work for perishable food, but also to seek for and receive the food which would endure through eternal life. To this they replied, "Lord, give us this bread." (John 6:34.) This was the setting in which Jesus made one of the greatest self-disclosures of all time. He referred to himself, saying, "I am the bread of life; he who comes to me shall not hunger, and he who believes in me shall never thirst." (John 6:35.)

Hungers of the Human Heart

Either the one who said "I am" ought to be followed with our complete allegiance, or else that man was the most self centered, egotistical, fanatical fool who ever lived and we ought to have nothing to do with him. But we do believe in the One who said, "I am the bread of life — I am the light of the world — I am the truth — I am the way." As we feast on him through faith, then the spiritual hungers of the human heart are satisfied. What are these hungers?

Hunger for Security

Basically there is a hunger for security. I am not talking about the type of security that a person seeks when he applies for a job. Our country was not built on that type of philosophy and it will not long endure on that type of a pension-security hunt. The security of which I speak is the desire to be loved, to know that someone cares. You can take much in the way of heartbreak and disappointment if you have one you know really loves you, in spite of your failures. Then you have a haven of rest and a place of peace.

Tiny babies, early in life, have the need to be loved. We raised four children, back in the days when you fed them by the clock — you know, every four hours! When our first child arrived we had to spend $2.98 of our $10.00 weekly pay in order to purchase a new clock with a good-workinq alarm. After all, that child had to be fed on schedule. He put up with this nonsense for awhile, but finally insisted on sleeping through his two a.m. meal. It was during these early days of frantic feeding that my wife insisted I join her in reading child psychology. Together we learned, if your child is a bottle-fed baby, you may use a bottle holder but don't overuse it. A baby, while being fed and having his physical needs satisfied, should have the feeling of security that comes from being held close to the body of a loved one. All of us are hungry for the security of knowing that someone holds us close because they care. we never outgrow this hunger. This longing to be loved is a vital part of each stage of life.

In the first two years at Haverford, Little Richard Kelly was passing out of the baby stage. Lois Kelly, a beautiful girl of nine, was the idol of her father and reciprocated his affection. After the silent Quaker meeting for worship one day, she told her mother she had spent the meeting hour deciding whom she loved best as she looked up at the gallery (where the elders of the meeting sit facing the meeting). After some weighing of the matter, she decided that she loved her daddy first, God second, Rufus Jones third, and J. Henry Bartlett fourth![1]

So much for Rufus Jones and Henry Bartlett, but how about getting "daddy" and God mixed up? Well how about it? The God I worship would smile down and say, "Thank goodness, I'm getting through, for there on the earth I have created through my humble and obedient servants a little colony of the kingdom of heaven where a young girl is learning the meaning of love." Lois Kelly was learning of her heavenly Father's love through the joy of receiving and responding to the love of her earthly father.

We were made for love. Life is stunted without it. The Japanese have a method of growing dwarfed trees. They take a little seedling that God meant to grow to be eighty or ninety feet tall in its mature years, and with a pair of scissors they sever the tap root. The tree in its lifespan is forced to live off the shallow surface roots. Even though it may be forty or fifty years old, it is only sixteen to eighteen inches high. This where man is today. Spiritually he is dwarfed. He may be a giant in terms of the technological world. He can send stars and missiles into the sky. He can orbit the earth and conquer outer space, while inner man is hungry for that which satisfied. Man is miserable until he finds fulfillment in love. Our lives are incomplete and unsatisfied until we learn and experience the joy of God's love for us in Christ.

[1]A bibliographical memoir by Douglas V. Steere in Thomas R. Kelly's, A Testament of Devotion (New York: Harper and Row Publishers, Inc., 1941). Used by permission. P. 17

Hungers of the Human Heart

A number of years ago I visited in London with Brigadier General Sir George Cockerill who, sixty years before, had led English expeditionary forces into India. I found he was an elderly man, very lonely, living in a mansion with just a housekeeper to care for him.After dinner, I listened to this man criticize my profession. He said, "Why don't you preachers get down to earth? Why don't you just tell your people that he is the God of love? And because he loved, he sent his Son. Jesus lived a way of love as no man has ever lived it. If the world only followed the example he set, it could know peace and security. Why do you preach theological nonsense which they don't understand and which, if they did, wouldn't make a bit of difference?" Then he got out a little book of sonnets in which he had revealed his life's philosophy. The title of his work was "Love's Universe." His thesis is profound in its simplicity. Let me summarize it for you:

This is Love's Universe. It was a
God of love who created it. He created us
in his image. He sent his Son to show us the
way. This Son, Jesus, lived a life of perfect
love. He never wavered even though it
meant death on a cross. If only we would
live that kind of life, loving one another as
he first loved us, the kingdom would come.

In the Bible we find these words, "I have loved you with an everlasting love; therefore, I have continued my faithfulness to you." (Jer. 31:3) Jesus said, "And I! when I am lifted up . . . will draw all men to myself." (John 12:32) Think of the magnetic power of the love of God in Christ! He is the living bread. If we feed on him, which is to live by his way of love, we will know the security of love. This is the hunger of the heart — a spiritual hunger that Christ can satisfy completely.

4

Hunger for Companionship

There is another hunger — the hunger for companionship. This is the desire to belong, not just to be a joiner but to belong to one another in creative, meaningful love relationships. We do not search for it. We only search for God — to know him, to love him, and to serve him — and fellowship and companionship come with it. Everyone of us has this hunger to belong. We want companionship in the spiritual realm, but until we know one another spiritually, we are not really close.

I remember when I was on a college campus, we worked at this thing. We worked at fellowship, but oh, how we worked at it! In the fraternity we held smoking parties. Our trouble was that when we concentrated on fellowship, we puffed so hard we couldn't see the fellows halfway across the room.

Do you know where I found real fraternity? I have found it in the church where ministers and laymen join together in the worship and service of the Almighty God. Our desire is to honor our Father and serve our brothers and sisters This has brought us satisfaction in our search for companionship. People are lonely and lives are incomplete until a worthy goal of life is found.

I have lived in Chicago and Los Angeles a total of fifteen years. There, as in other major cities, live millions of people. The masses of men rub shoulders. Sometimes you can hardly walk across the street. You are pushed on either more in front, and behind. So many people and so many of them are so desperately lonely! Even in a crowd one can be lonely of heart — starved for companionship.

One of our magazines a few years ago sent out a questionnaire. They were working at this thing from a little different angle. They sent the form to over two hundred men whom they assumed were still happily married. This questionnaire — and I'm for more like it — had just one question to be answered. It said, "Gentlemen, what have you discovered is the best way to hold on to your wife?" Well, evidently the men weren't too sure of themselves. They only received one reply. This came from a midwestern penitentiary. The fellow said, "Dear Sirs, I discovered that the best way to hold a wife is around the neck, but it can easily be overdone. P. S Please note change of address." The mere proximity of the physical is insufficient to satisfy the deeper longings of the spiritual.

I believe we need family altars where persons are drawn close to God and to one another. This can be a hallowed place in the home. But, of course, an altar is not so much a place or thing as it is an attitude of the heart.

'Mid all the traffic of the ways,
Turmoils without, within,
Make in my heart a quiet place,
And come and dwell therein:

A little shrine of quietness,
All sacred to Thyself,
Where Thou shalt all my soul possess,
And I may find myself.[2]

—John Oxenham

One Sunday night following a sermon entitled "The Family Altar," we had a special meeting of our official board to care for an emergency matter. After the meeting one of my fine laymen came up and said, 'I'd like to talk to you for a few minutes. I've been thinking about what you said this morning. I believe the only thing for me to do is to resign from the official board. You see, we don't have a family altar. My own children have never heard me read a word of scripture; they have never heard me breathe a word of prayer. I don't deserve to be on the official board." I offered my services to come to his home to help get a family altar started. He said, I'd like that, but my wife wouldn't." Later in the week I saw his wife at a Woman's meeting. She came up and said, "Could I please see you?

[2]"Sanctuary" from the vision Splendid by John Oxenham. Used by permission of Miss Theo Oxenham.

I'm very disturbed about what you said Sunday morning. What you don't realize is that what seems easy for you who preach from the pulpit is difficult for us as laypersons." She went on to tell me that they had no family altar. Again I offered to help. And she said, "No, I would like that, but my husband wouldn't."

Were they married? Did they belong to each other? Was there a feeling of companionship between them? They had a marriage license. They could prove they were married. They were living under the same roof and eating at the same table. They were sleeping in the same bed. Physical union had produced children Yes, they were married. But yet I maintain that any man and wife who cannot talk about the deep hungers of the spirit, one with the other, are not married in the deepest sense of the word. In a number of years, God worked in his wonderful way. Something happened to these two people. You could see it in their faces. They became great leaders in that church. They became companions of the Spirit.

We have a longing to belong. We are hungry for a creative companionship that is born and nurtured of the spirit of God. Do we find it? We find it as we seek together that which God alone can reveal through his Son — the elder Brother of our faith.

Jesus taught us to pray, "Our Father ..." He is the Father of us all. We need to learn to live together as companions before there can be joy in our own hearts and homes and peace in the world.

Hunger for Achievement

Another hunger of the human heart is the hunger for achievement. The hunger for achievement is the desire to be serving. This is the desire to contribute in time that which will outlast time. All of us are hungry to know that we are contributing something significant and eternal

Some of us may be leaders and others may be followers. Faithful followership is as necessary as good leadership. In building the kingdom of God, everyone has something to do, something to contribute that he alone can do. We ought to enter into this business of living with a sense of mission and purpose — with a holy excitement.

Did you hear the story about one of our more fashionable colleges for women? It seems the dean sent out a questionnaire to parents of incoming freshmen girls. On the list was a question, "Is your daughter a good leader?" Evidently the parents all answered. The dean wrote a letter to one humble couple and said, "My dear friends, we're so glad you're sending your daughter to be a member of the freshman class. Inasmuch as the class is going to number at least 215 girls and we already are assured of 214 good leaders, we are glad your daughter is coming along to be a follower."

Paul said to the Romans, "I bid every one among you not to think of himself more highly than he ought to think." This is sound advice. But the Bible also makes clear that every man's life shall count. No one is insignificant in the sight of God. All are important. It speaks of man as being just a little lower than the angels. This is vastly different than saying he is a little higher than the devil! Every man is called to be a faithful steward of his life and of his possessions. There must be a balanced relationship between not thinking too highly of one's self but yet modestly thinking of one's self as contributing one's best to God's kingdom. No one should ever belittle his best. It is God's gift.

Some years ago in Vincennes, Indiana, I stayed in a rooming house and walked uptown to have my breakfast before addressing a district meeting for ministers. I walked by a very small business establishment. To this day I can see it. Two men had formed a partnership, and here they sold peanuts, gum, the daily newspaper, and so on. The amazing thing about this shop was that you saw as you walked along, up in the gable just below the roof, a neatly printed sign. The same message was on both sides. I read the message and chuckled to myself. What do you suppose these two men, operating this modest business in this tiny establishment, were saying to the world via this painted sign? They said, "We occupy the whole building." God asks us to do the best we can with what we have and what we are. When we do this, we feel a sense of real mission. The part we play in the drama of redemption is important. It pleases God, helps our Philemon, and satisfies our own souls. If we will only make our investment in service, he will satisfy this hunger we have for real achievement.

There are people on the other side of the street and on the other side of the nation and on the other side of the world who are helping; they are those who some time during the day bow before God and say, "Father, I am yours. Use me this day." Knowing this gives us a new sense of deep optimism which is good because it fulfills a basic hunger. Jesus is always calling us. He has said, "Follow me, and I will make you fishers of men." (Matt. 4:19 K.J.V.) This is life's greatest privilege. All of life ought to be permeated with the spirit of Christ so that we are fishers and trainers of men.

In the First World War many had been out in the front lines for several days and nights with no sleep and little food. They were weary wet, and battle fatigued when they heard reinforcements coming from the rear. The replacement captain said to the captain of the worn and weary group, "Go back to rest camp. About midway back you'll find a little Salvation Army hut. There's a lovely young lady there. She'll have some steaming hot coffee for the boys." The assurance of a cup of hot coffee, and the sight of a pretty, smiling girl perked them up. When they arrived, the men lined up automatically, army style, each grabbing a great big crocker cup. The girl started pouring from a steaming pot of coffee. She had poured only a few cups when the chaplain's assistant said, "Stop pouring the coffee. We're going to bow our heads and thank Jesus that the boys have come back." She kept serving the coffee because the men were cold and tired. In a few moments he again said, "Stop pouring the coffee. Let's thank Jesus that the boys have come back." The next fellow in the line, having watched her at work, said quietly, "Sir, you don't understand. She puts Jesus in every cup." We too are to put the spirit of Christ into the cup of everyday living. Each one can become a fisher of men and a teacher of men. This is to achieve. We may never arrive, but we can serve and contr bute in time that which will outlast time. People are hungry for this kind of achievement.

Hunger for Recognition

Finally, we hunger for recognition. This is the desire to be noticed — to be recognized. When Jesus came up out of the River Jordan following his baptism, his Father said, "This is my beloved Son, in whom I am well pleased." (Matt. 3:17 K. J. V.) No wonder he could go into the wilderness and remain loyal when tempted! He had heard his Father say that he was pleased. This is spiritual recognition.

There is something mysterious about the peace that spiritual recognition can bring. A man of my parish had been sick. I had seen him out on the farm a number of times. When he went to the hospital for surgery, they could do nothing. They said he would live a number of months — maybe a year. He knew it was diagnosed as incurable cancer. He went home for his remaining days. One morning I went to my study to read and meditate, but I couldn't get him out of my mind. I felt I should go see him. No , I was just out there recently. This morning I'll study and go to see him this afternoon. But the mental urging continued, so I finally picked up the phone and called. The daughter said, "Don't bother to come. Dad is in a deep coma. He didn't even recognize the doctor who was just here." I said, "I want to come." When I got there, I sat down in a chair by his bed. His hand was lying limp. I put my hand over his and, speaking his name clearly, told him who had come to see him. His hand gripped mine weakly. I prayed for him. After a prayer of commitment, he reverently murmured a quiet, "Thank you"; his eyelids closed and his hand released. In less than three hours he had passed away. It was not anything I had done, but the work of the One I am privileged to represent. Everyone needs this benediction of approval from above.

These desires, the deep longings, are more than psychological. They are spiritual hungers and can only be satisfied with spiritual food as we feast on Christ through faith in our hearts and lives. He said "I am the bread of life." He came not to destroy but to fulfill in love.

We are hungry for security. We have the desire to love and be loved, to know that someone cares. Christ revealed the extent of God's love for us. We have a hunger for companionship. We want to belong to one another in meaningful, creative, love relationships. Then too, Jesus, our elder brother says, "You are my friends." He accepts us as we are and helps us become what we were meant to be. Oh, how satisfying! We have a hunger for achievement, a desire to be serving, to contribute in time that which will outlast time. As we follow Christ who said, "Follow me, and I will make you fishers of men," we find that hunger fulfilled. We have a hunger for recognition, a desire to be noticed, not only to be approved by one another on earth but to feel the approval of God from on high. If we will live the right, good, moral, and spiritual life, we will hear these words in one way or another, "This is my beloved Son, in whom I am well pleased." Thus will life be fulfilled.

It is Christ who is the "bread of life." He satisfies the the hungers of the human heart. He alone makes the difference.

> 'Twas battered and scarred, and the auctioneer
> Thought it scarcely worth his while
> To waste much time on the old violin,
> But he held it up with a smile
> "What am I bidden, good folks," he cried,
> "Who will start bidding for me?
> A dollar, a dollar" — then, "Two!" "Only two?
> Two dollars, and who'll make it three
> Three dollars, once, three dollars, twice;
> Going for three—" But no,
> From the room far back, a gray-haired man
> Came forward and picked up the bow;
> Then, wiping the dust from the old violin,
> And tightening the loose strings,
> He played a melody pure and sweet
> As sweet as a caroling angel sings.

Hungers of the Human Heart

> The music ceased, and the auctioneer,
> With a voice that was quiet and low,
> Said,"What am I bidden for the old violin?"
> And he held it up with the bow.
> "A thousand dollars, and who'll make it two?
> Two thousand! and Who'll make it three?
> Three thousand, once; three thousand, twice;
> And going, and gone!" said he.
> The people cheered, but some of them cried,
> "We do not quite understand.
> What changed its worth?" Swift came the reply:
> "The touch of the master's hand."
>
> And many a man with life out of tune,
> And battered and scarred with sin,
> Is auctioned cheap to the thoughtless crowd,
> Much like the old violin.
> A "mess of pottage," a glass of wine ;
> A game — and he travels on.
> He's "going" once, and "going" twice,
> He's "going" and "almost gone."
> But the Master comes, and the foolish crowd
> Never can quite understand
> The worth of a soul, and the change that's wrought
> By the touch of the Master's hand.[3]

- Myra Brooks Welch

[3]"The Touch of the Master's Hand." Copyright 1943 by the Brethren Press. Used by permission.

Hungers of the Human Heart

Hungers of the Human Heart

Chapter Two
Life's Eternal Question
What shall I do with Jesus?" — Matt. 27:22

Jesus had been captured. The dastardly plot was successful. They had taken him from place to place and now he was before Pilate. Pilate was not exactly a young upstart in this business of handling men and knowing people. He did not have to have a wife to dream that this man was innocent. He knew Jesus. His wife just verified his own verdict. On this feast day when, as was their custom, the people could ask for the release of one of the prisoners, Pilate undoubtedly arranged for them to see the great difference between Jesus and Barabbas, a notorious prisoner. He stood Jesus and Barabbas before the crowd and asked them, "Whom do you want me to release for you, Barabbas or Jesus who is called Christ?" They shouted, "Barabbas." Then he said, "What shall I do with Jesus?" They all cried, "Let him be crucified." And he said, "Why, what evil has he done?" That question was never answered. Mobs never answer questions. "They shouted all the more, 'Let him be crucified!'" And Pilate released Barabbas and delivered Jesus to be crucified. (Matt. 27:15-26.)

Man's eternal question is: "What shall I do with Jesus?" We all must do something with him. Once we have heard anything about his life, his teachings and gospel, his death and resurrection, we must do something. Jesus is the eternal contemporary. Every generation must answer this question: What shall I do with Jesus? It haunts us. Sometimes people try to bluff their way, but there is no bluffing in answering this question.

Perhaps you've heard of the boy in school who never prepared his homework, but he had a way of tickling the ego of the teacher and she'd take off and lecture the rest of the period. Finally the teacher "wised up" and one day she asked little Johnny a question. He sort of looked off into space and said, "I don't think I know. What do you think?" The teacher replied, "I don't think — I know!" The boy then said, "That's just it. I don't think I know, either." Since the beginning of time, man has had to wrestle with important questions. He cannot successfully evade them. The question posed by our text is the most urgent.

I Can Reject Him

There are at least four answers to this eternal question. First, I can reject him. Francis of Assisi said, "God is always courteous and never invades the privacy of the human soul " A painting by Holman Hunt portrays Jesus gently knocking at a door. The latch is on the inside. If we hear him knocking and hear his voice and open the door, he will come in and eat with us and we with him. (Rev. 3:20.) But we must first open the door. God, though he is Almighty, still is gracious and never invades the privacy of the human soul.

I remember going to a church one time and, in the process of getting acquainted with some of the leaders, went into a home where the wife was very active in church affairs. Her husband was not a member of the church. I was in that home less than three minutes when that man, in a very self-centered, satisfied, successful, egotistical tone of voice, said that he had "gotten the best of my predecessor in a theological debate." I doubted that. I knew my predecessor. He was a great man of God, and it was a joy to come and try to build on the foundation he had so thoroughly laid in that congregation and parish. I had to say to this most successful man-he had two TV sets before most of us could have one — he had

16

two fancy cars and then bought a third one — "I haven't come here to debate religion. I just want you to know that I love my Lord. He's been mighty good to me. I love the fellowship of the church. There's nothing like it on earth. And I've come to share with you people of this community what Christ means to me and how much I appreciate the ministry of the Master through the church." Then I said, "If, at any time, you'd like me to be your pastor as well as your wife's pastor, just let me know. I'll be ready." This is the best one can do when dealing with a person who is rejecting God.

Little did he know that, before I had completed my first year in that church, he would suffer a coronary thrombosis and be rushed to the hospital. In those agonizing hours his wife remembered what her minister had said. There had been no arguments. There had been no hard feelings. There had simply been the open door of the pastor, who had said he would come if ever wanted. Now when her husband was seriously ill, she reminded him of what the minister had said and asked: "Honey, would you like for me to send for him now?" "Please do," he answered.

When I went into the hospital room he was in an oxygen tent. He was no longer self-sufficient and eager to argue religion. Here was a man humble and scared to death. He was ready to turn to God. Let's never make fun of "fox-hole" religion. I'm just glad and grateful there is a God to whom we can go even though we reject him until the very last. He's that kind of loving Father. I slipped my hand into the opening of the tent and said, quietly, "I'm glad you sent for me. It is a privilege to talk with you and God. I'll pray and pause after each sentence. You think the words and make them your prayer, and then, regardless of how this situation turns out, you'll be all right. Because whether it's life here or life over there, it's all life with God." I prayed. He smiled and thanked me I left. Before morning he was gone.

It has been my experience in working with people who have been atheistic or who have rejected God that they have only assumed this role when life was apparently going quite well without him, or so they thought. When a crisis arises or a man is "scared to

17

death," he instinctively turns to God.

I Can Neglect Him

The second response or answer to this eternal question, "What shall I do with Jesus?" is, I can neglect him. While I would not consciously think of rejecting him, I can and do just that. I mean to put God and his church first in my life, but I never quite get around to it. Someday I am going to — but not just yet. So we give the odds and ends of our time and the loose change in our pocket when we occasionally attend church. We call that and ourselves Christian.

There is a story told of a man who was very busy down here on earth. He tried to get into heaven when he died. They asked him, "What did you think of our world down there?" The poor fellow had to say, "I'm sorry, I didn't see it. I was busy telephoning." How many of us are busy telephoning! Many times we have heard people say, "I would do this for my God, for my church, but I gust don't have the time. I would like to have an hour for daily meditation, but I don't have time. I would like to attend church regularly, but I'm just too busy." This is not a statement of fact! It is a judgment of value. What we are really saying is that we don't think it is quite as important as most of the other things we do.

We are living in a culture that is more gadget-minded than God- minded. It is easy to let the nonessentials clutter up our daily living. At best we major in minors, giving primary allegience to secondary matters. Once while calling in the home of church members I learned that neither husband nor wife had made a financial pledge. Although both had good paying positions and there were no children to support, and in spite of the fact that they had made a sacred vow at the altar, they said that they preferred not to pledge and pay regularly as they never knew for sure what their incomes would be. It was interesting to observe in the course of our conversation, however, that even though they already had three toasters, they had just gotten a new one.

Some years from now there will be a float in a parade depicting our generation. It will be most beautiful and colorful. Those riding on the float will all have their eyes fixed on what appears to be the object of devotion and worship. It is on the highest pinnacle. Low and behold, it is an automatic pop-up toaster, going pop, pop, pop! It will say to the world that we were participants in a materialistic culture. We were more interested in pleasure than in purpose. We were more mindful of the pursuit of gadgets than of the pursuit of God.

Do you think this an exaggeration? Then let me tell you of a double murder which took place in Phoenix, Arizona. The victims were not shot. Both husband and wife were slain with a knife. The man was found in the bedroom. The woman was found on the davenport in the living room. Her feet had been tied together. Her hands were fastened behind her back. She had been nearly decapitated when they slashed her throat. But they were very thoughtful. They were very careful, these mad, crazed killers! Before they cut her throat they unfolded magazines and several newspapers, putting them under her head and shoulders so the blood wouldn't soil the davenport. Even mad killers protect property while destroying life!

What about us? Is God as revealed in Christ really in the seat of power? Is he really making the decisions? Do spiritual values and those things belonging to the Kingdom come first? Or do we just talk about him and then shut him off, as we do a TV program we don't particularly like, and enjoy the materialistic culture of our lives? What shall I do with Jesus? Shall I neglect him?

Little Nancy had heard the Christmas story over and over, so one day she said, "Mommy, can I read it?" She just couldn't stand it that there was no room at the inn for the baby Jesus and Mary, his mother, so when she came to the place where Joseph knocked at the innkeeper's door, she read it like this, "Good evening, sir. My wife is going to have a baby tonight She needs a place to stay. Could you make room for us here?" The innkeeper said, "Well our place is crowded, but there is always room for one more. Come on in," Nancy gleefully exclaimed, "That's a better way to tell it, isn't it, Mommy?"

> Let not our hearts be busy inns,
> That have no room for Thee,
> But cradles for the living Christ
> And His Nativity.[1]

I Can Accept Him

What shall I do with Jesus? I do not want to reject or even neglect him. I shall accept him When we accept him, things change. Life is reoriented. Everything takes on a new purpose, a new direction. A man would look pretty silly if he took his boat up to the dock, threw the rope over, and tried to pull the dock to the boat. Yet how many times we pray, "God help me," instead of saying, "What is it you want me to do?"

Arnold Toynbee, who has painted the rise and fall of many nations and has revealed the fact that the seeds of destruction have already been sown in ours, was once asked if there was any hope of survival for our civilization. He indicated that there is hope — if man will become adjusted to the eternal. To accept Christ and his way of life is to accept the will of the eternal God. When this is done, life has a direction in humble and joyful service. Change comes to the world because change has come to people.

We're told that in Missouri there is a community not known exactly for its liberal outlook on any issue. The school board of this community was looking for a new school teacher. They had a likely candidate whom they were interviewing, and finally the chairman of the board "lowered the boom" and asked the big question for that community. He said, "Ma'am, what do you consider the shape of the world?" "What do you mean, sir?" she inquired. The man asked, "Do you think it is round or flat?" To this she replied, "I'm not quite sure, but I'm prepared to teach it either way." The school board

[1]Ralph Spaulding Cushman. A Pocket Prayer Book (Nashville: The upper Room, 1941), p. 98.

adjourned and met for awhile in another room; then they returned and said, "You're hired, but we prefer that you teach the old flat theory since we don't think it would be wise to introduce anything new in this community." If we accept God, known through Christ, then we will adjust to him and there will be plenty of revolutionary changes. There will even be changes in the church. Then and only then will we have the power to go out and create a culture and civilization in which God can be pleased. What shall I do with Jesus? I will accept him and make the necessary changes and let love — sacrificial, self-denying love — and joyful service be that which will guide the rest of my days.

I Can Surrender to Him

What shall I do with Jesus? I will accept him and surrender myself to him. Not reject. Not neglect. Not only accept, but surrender. By and large we do not like the word "surrender." Most men will remember when they were young and wrestled with the neighbor boys. Sometimes they would get us down and shout, "Give up? Do you give up?" We would rather take a beating before we would give up. And yet, not until man surrenders in the great wrestling match of life does he ever experience the joy of victory. You have to give up to win. Whenever man becomes surrendered, then he wins, and he lives.

A man asked three of the great world Christians, separately, the same question: "If you had to name one word that best described the secret of your success, what would that word be?" Muriel Lester said, "Surrender." E. Stanley Jones and Tokyo Kagawa said, "Surrender." The great souls of the past and present who have found victory in life and joy with Christ have surrendered.

Surrendering is a process. Sometimes we feel that we are getting a little closer and then, in some subtle, almost unconscious way, we discover that we are far from it. We need always to remind ourselves that the joy of victory comes in surrender. It is not enough to look to Jesus and to the cross and say, "He surrendered all. He died, completely giving his all for our sins." We must answer the haunting question of Pilate, "What shall I do with Jesus?" One day the author went into a Sunday school class and the children were reciting what they had learned about Jesus. After re-citing a long list, one little fellow stood up and said, "I think we ought to do something for Jesus." It isn't enough to just look at Jesus and say, "Look what he has done for us?" Ours is the privilege of doing something for him. The surrender of self in loving devotion is our finest gift.

A young lad in Washington, D. C., seeing the magnificent Lincoln Memorial, stood in awe looking at the kindly, compassionate face of the great man. He had studied history and civics and understood something of the passion of this president's to desire to free the slaves. A man passed and asked, "What do you think of him, sonny?" There was a long pause Evidently the lad was so absorbed he never heard the question. It was repeated. The young fellow thoughtfully, even reverently answered, "I want to be like him." We can say this about Christ. It is not enough to know of him and teach about him. We can become like him, completely surrendered to the will of God revealed through him.

In the excitement of a state basketball tournament, a man with a microphone found the captain of the winning team and asked if he was surprised with the state championship. He said, "No." The man then asked the coach if he was surprised. Again the answer was "No." He went on to explain, "Early in the season we knew we had the makings of a good ball club. The boys and I got together and decided that this year we intended to go all the way." That inner spirit of intention to go all the way made the team impossible to beat. From the moment of deep resolve they were headed for victory. Their resolve meant the surrender of many petty, selfish desires. Each member of the team had committed himself to the keeping of rigid training rules. This surrender had not destroyed life for them but rather had prepared them for a greater victory.

Man's eternal question continues to confront us. What shall I do with Jesus? Shall I reject him? Surely, no! Shall I neglect him?

I pray not. Shall I accept him? Yes, this is my desire. And furthermore, knowing that I have complete control over my own will, I pray that my acceptance of Christ shall lead to my surrender to him. Then God will bless me with the joy of everlasting victory!

Hungers of the Human Heart

Chapter Three
What the World Needs Now

"Love one another"— John 4:7

Hal David and Burt Bacharach have given us a song, "What The World Needs Now is Love..." Their thinking is straight when they indicate that this love "is not just for some but for everyone."

I once heard a president of a university, in referring to a certain student, say, "He's a nice fellow, but he is missing what is important. He is majoring in the minors, yet acts like he is mastering the curriculum." If we are to master the curriculum of living and meet the needs of our world there will be a new conviction to that which is really important, there will be a depth of consecration becoming to those whose priorities are right, and there will be a new level of compassion which is our expression of love.

Conviction

Bishop Gerald Kennedy relates the story of the convention of atheists which was addressed by one of the delegates who was complaining about their half-hearted enthusiasm for atheism. He concluded his speech with these words: "Thank God! I am a real atheist!"

25

Hungers of the Human Heart

This mixed up befuddled world of ours needs people with real conviction concerning that which is important. My friend, the late Dr. Harold Bosley, who spent his life in the church said of it, "She has great convictions about little problems and little convictions about great problems." To the degree that this is true of any institution it is tragic. The cult of conformity and our unwillingness toengage in costly encounter, all for the sake of a false peace and quiet, can be disastrous.

Our extreme individualistic commercialism is selfish. Why continue to use men to make money when we can use money to make men? We are in a people's business, but to use people for selfish gain is not only unchristian, it is inhuman. What the world needs now is people who have conviction about the importance of persons over property and possessions.

I will always remember an extended conversation with Dr. Albert Schweitzer concerning the bomb. He and Albert Einstein had covenanted that whoever was left would continue to wage war against the bomb and nuclear proliferation. One wonders when we will become sufficiently of age around the world so that we will be filled with discontent spending billions of dollars for war while we invest pennies for peace. And this in a world where hundreds of millions go to bed hungry every night and thousands die of starvation daily. I have been in Calcutta and walked the streets at daybreak to see the bodies of those who had slipped away during the night picked up and carted away. Smiley Blanton in this book, "Love or Perish," states it succinctly, "Love is no luxury." This is true individually, and it is true corporately. If we have conviction concerning the use of the resources God has given us we will move to alleviate human suffering and provide technical assistance to help the people of undeveloped nations to get on their own feet.

There are differences of opinion concerning the use of alcohol as a beverage. Most would agree, however, that there is something wrong with the value system of a nation whose people spend three times as much for alcohol as for all churches. Way back in the Old Testament is the practically forgotten book of Habakkuk. This so-called minor prophet lived and served some six hundred years before the time of Christ. We know he dwelt in the midst of a sinful people. Despair was very much a part of their everyday attitude. Immorality was rampant. Those who wanted to believe in God were disillusioned. How could there be a God when these, his people, were so troubled? When it looked as though all hope was gone of ever developing a righteousness that would be adequate for survivalHabakkuk as it were, climbed the ladder of faith and, looking into the face of God, prayed. This is the power of any prophet in any time. He is not content to stay in the mire of the day in which he lives, but he climbs his ladder of faith and, looking into the eyes of God or kneeling at the foot of the cross, he prays. And Habakkuk prayed, "O Lord, revive thy work." If there ever is going to be a new day it must begin with prayer. John R. Mott, who toured the world many times strengthening mission work, said that wherever in the world he saw things happening to build the kingdom of God, when he looked into it, he found that someone had prayed. Prayer produces power for constructive change.

Habakkuk also says, "The Lord is in his holy temple: Let all the earth keep silence before him." (Hab. 2:20 K. J. V.) But Habakkuk would never have us think that we can just find God in his holy temple and stay there. No, he would say, "Pray for God's guidance." Then he would say, "Go out and serve." Be a part of the answer to the prayer that you have just prayed.

Concerning the misuse of alcohol Habakkuk wrote:

> Woe to him who makes his neighbors drink of the
> cup of his wrath, and makes them drunk, to gaze on
> their shame! You will be sated with contempt instead
> of glory. Drink, yourself, and stagger! The cup in the
> Lord's right hand will come around to you, and shame
> will come upon your glory!
>
> - Hab. 2:15-16

We are told that fifty percent of the traffic fatalities are caused by the drinking driver. Think of the shame and heartache! It is high time we have some conviction concerning this waste.

Integrity is more than just a word in the dictionary. If it is wrong to cheat and lie, we had better have some conviction about it. William Van Orsdell was known as Brother Van. He served as an itinerant preacher during the pioneer days of early America. One day he was talking to some Indians who were to journey with him to visit another man. They put all their belongings, including Brother Van's, in another man's tepee. Brother Van said to one of them, "This is everything in the world I own. Is this safe?" The Indian replied, "There isn't a white man within a hundred miles. It's perfectly safe!" Are we really honest — genuine and sincere? Can people count on our word as being completely true? It is still a tribute to be able to say of a person, "He's as honest as the day is long. His word is as good as gold."

One of the most difficult problems I ever had came early in my ministry as a result of my announcing that we were planning to have an all-church picnic on a Sunday afternoon. I didn't see anything wrong with it. We were to have Sunday school and worship as usual. Everyone was encouraged to bring a basket lunch. All would go over to a nearby state park right after the service so we could eat and fellowship together. Well, one family in that church tried to run me out of town. Think of a preacher being an agent of the devil, leading his flock straight to hell — planning a picnic on Sunday! In those "good old days" some Methodists were a mite more strict than we are nowadays. Nevertheless I didn't think it was wrong. I thought we could have good Christian fellowship together as a church family. Oh, what trouble they caused! I did the only thing I knew to do. I went to see this man and his wife who were "raising cain." Cain is a polite word. I called on a Sunday afternoon as I wanted to be sure to find the entire family at home. The mother, embarrassed, met me at the door. Her husband came in. He was flustered. You never feel comfortable, you know, when you meet face to face the person you've been criticizing. I asked where the children were as I wanted the family together. Then their faces did get red! The kids weren't there. Where do you suppose they were? They were at the theater attending a Sunday afternoon matinee! Sharp tongues, bitter critical attitudes for others, but they had allowed their own children to go and support a commercial amusement on a Sunday afternoon.

You would not give two cents for a preacher who didn't have some convictions. You would rather disagree with him sometimes than have him so lackadaisical that you never knew where he stood. Do you want a preacher who waits to see what happens in his community and then echoes the popular voice? No, most people want their leader to be a voice — not an echo. I'm reminded of a pastoral relations committee that was looking for a preacher. They went to the bishop. He asked, "Now just what kind of a man do you want?" "Well," said the committee chairman, "you used to send us shouters, now you send us whisperers. Can't you send us something in between?"

The world is in dire need of more leaders and members of the serving institutions who have a proper blending of humility and the courage of conviction to stand up and be counted! There will never be a new day until the moral climate is right. From the Diary of Jonathan Edwards we find an example of the determination we need:

Resolved: that every man should live to the glory of God.
Resolved Second: that whether others do this or not, I will.[1]
To have burning convictions on the important issues of life and to become involved in what is really significant will do two things. It will bless others
for whom we are concerned and it will help us discover the true meaning of life.

Revival of Consecration

The second thing we need is a depth of consecration. It is

[1]Cushman, op. cit., p. 23.a

not enough just to have conviction. There needs to be a real deep-seated consecration. This is love in action. We, like Habakkuk, can pray, "Lord, revive thy work," and then develop the deep desire within to express the love of God in everyday life. God has given us the gift of his Son, the One who lived a life of perfect love. Let us become consecrated to him. Then it will happen. A real witness of right religion will take place. Whenever we present the Master of love, people know that we care, and lives are changed. We too are blessed.

One of the most beautiful letters I ever received came from a young couple in a church I had just left. They didn't know how to say it, but they wanted to thank their former minister for what had happened to them. After several attempts at stating it, they simply wrote, "Thank you for introducing us to Jesus." When they found Jesus, they found love. Their home, once on a shaky foundation, was now a Christian home. Their life became filled with love. Their once aloof attitude toward the church became a burning, flaming passion for the institution whose service had brought new life to them. This is what happens when love moves in and takes over. Everything falls into proper relationship.

A God of love created us to love and serve one another. If we love one another as Christ has loved us, the kingdom will come.

> A picket frozen on duty,
> A mother starved for her brood,
> Socrates drinking the hemlock,
> And Jesus on the rood;
> And millions who, humble and nameless,
> The straight, hard pathway plod —
> Some call it Consecration,
> And others call it God.[2]

How can you separate it when the consecration is in God and of

[2] William Herbert Carruth, "Each in His Own Tongue," from Each in His Own Tongue and Other Poems G. P. Putnam's Son, 200 Madison Ave., N.Y. 16 N.Y.

God? There should be in us the burning passion to become consecrated. Frances R. Havergal has written helpful words:

Take my life, and let it be
Consecrated, Lord, to Thee.
Take my moments and my days;
Let them flow in ceaseless praise.

Take my hands, and let them move
At the impulse of Thy love.
Take my feet, and let them be
Swift and beautiful for Thee.

To respond to the impulse of the Father's love and conse-
crate ourselves to the mission of bringing everyone in right relationship with him is life's most glorious privilege.

We had a group of young people at our cabin in Canada
some summers ago. In the mornings we had an informal program,
during which time we set aside one block of forty-five minutes which
we called "The Big Idea." At that time everyone sought a solitary
spot. Each could take his Bible if he wished. Or he could take a
notebook and write, but he had to be alone. I can see them yet: one
out on a rock dangling his feet in the water, some sitting on the edge
of the dock, another leaning up against a big white pine or settled
among the white birch trees. These young people were contemplat-
ing, "What is the Big idea in my life today?" Following this time of
creative quiet, we gathered to share our big ideas. They were tre-
mendous! Do you have a big idea?

I want to have the big idea of letting God have his way in my
life. I want to let the love of Christ shine through me so that others,
through my humble efforts, might learn to know him and say, 'Thank
you for introducing us to Jesus." Would not this be a big idea for all
of us — to become consecrated,committed to the extension of
God's kingdom of love? There will never be much of a new day of
discovery until we go deeper in personal commitment to God; then

we can rise higher in character and go further toward world peace.

Compassion

Finally, if there is to be a new day there will need to be in us a new depth of compassion for all humanity. This is the deeper love which expresses itself in service for others, for the right reasons. The world is in need of a mighty quest for greatness. Good needs to be done, not because it is politically expedient, but simply because we care. Jesus set the example. He had compassion and went about doing good.

Charles H. Malik, former President of The United Nations General Assembly, an active Lebanese Eastern Orthodox Churchman, said it well:

> We — all of us — need a mighty spiritual revival. The ideal successful, selfish life is wholly inadequate. One craves to see great themes sought and discussed, great causes espoused. One burns for the reintroduction into life of the pursuit of greatness. Everywhere I go I find people sitting on the edges of their seats waiting to be shown the way. There are infinite possibilities, both material and moral, to vindicate freedom against unfreedom, joy of living against tyranny, man against all that is sub-human and inhuman, truth against darkness and falsehood, and God against the devil and his works. The time is here, not for pessimism and despair, but for a vast advance on many fronts.[3]

The time is past due for our pursuit of greatness. The deep hungers of the heart will never be satisfied if we continue to fill our lives with trivial things nor will civilization be saved. Deeds of love

[3]Charles H. Malik. Reprinted from This Week Magazine. Copyright 1960 by United Newspapers Magazine Corporation. Used by permission.

will help to save the day and give us cause for a wholesome optimism. The good Samaritan had it; that is why we call him good. The priest and Levite were nice respectable people. The only trouble was they were no doubt too occupied running the ecclesiastical machinery. They were busy having meetings. Meetings will not do alone. It is the witness that does it. Sometimes we witness in very humble and yet very effective ways. The good Samari-tan went and bound up the wounds. He took the man to the inn and paid for his care. Furthermore he added, "Take care of him; and whatever more you spend, I will repay you when I come back." We call him the good Samaritan because, like the Master, he had compassion. (Luke 10:25-37.)

In the nineteenth chapter of Luke we find Jesus coming up to Jerusalem. "When he drew near and saw the city he wept over it, saying, 'Would that even today you knew the things that make for cumin, '" (Luke 19:42-42.) Jesus cared so much that his heart ached and he wept because the people were living in sin and they would not hear his word. And he said, "Woe to you, scribes and Pharisees, hypocrites! For you tithe mint and dill and cumin, and have neglected the weightier matters of the law, justice and mercy and faith; these you ought to have done, without neglecting the others." (Matt. 23:23.) How much do we care for people? Do we have compassion for them?

You have a neighbor living across the street and you never befriend him. It is no use waiting until that neighbor dies and then contribute for flowers. That is not compassion. That is just a little respect. Let your neighbor know you care. Do your best and God will do the rest.

Compassion is contagious. When Dwight L. Moody was in his prime he went to England to preach a series of meetings. A great preacher over there, R. W. Dale, was openly opposed to his coming because Moody was an "out and out evangelist." But Dale's people went to hear Moody. Finally they began to come and say, "Dr. Dale, you have to come and hear this man. He is not like you think he is."   And so one night Dr. Dale heard Dwight L. Moody.

Hungers of the Human Heart

After that he went back night after night as long as Moody was in England. Someone asked, "Why did you go back when you at first were so opposed?" He said, "Because Dwight L. Moody could not talk about a lost soul without a tear in his eye. Anyone who loves people that much, I will gladly hear." Unless there is a tear in the heart, if not a tear in the eye, for those who are outside the Kingdom of love ! we will never do much in meeting the real needs, the inner heart — hungers, of people. We don't have to be profound to do this, just loving and real. It is not so much what we say, but how we live that counts. Mr. Stanley said of David Livingston, after having met him in Africa, "It was not Livingston's preaching that converted me, it was Livingston's living."

Paul probably never saw Christ in the flesh, but he surely met him. He opened his heart to let him in and from then on Paul was a channel through which the passion and love and concern of Christ flowed. What a power he was! In writing to the Colossians he said, "This is the Christ we proclaim; we train everyone and teach everyone the full scope of this knowledge, in order to set everyone before God mature in Christ." (Col. 1:28 Moffatt) There is the goal — Christlike maturity — that everyone might stand before God mature in Christ, not spiritual dwarfs but mature in the faith. After Paul thus defined the goal he says of himself.

"I labor for that end, striving for it with the divine energy which is a power within me. Striving? Yes, I want you to understand my deep concern for you, for those at Laodicea, and for all who have never seen my face. May their hearts be encouraged! May they learn the meaning of love! May they have all the wealth of conviction that comes from insight." (Col. 1:29-2:2 Moffatt)

How many people do you suppose have learned the true meaning of love? If people know that we have a burning desire to set everyone before God mature in Christ, they will be blest. Our efforts will bear fruit. It is the proclaiming of the good news of God's love in Christ. When we tell "the old, old story of Jesus and his love" and make effective witness of our faith, we are on the way to real religion. This is the desperate need of our world today.

We are in need of experiencing and expressing conviction, conse-cration, and compassion. We all want to see this world saved from a great war that would destroy civilization. We all want to see a world in which peoplea, will live together as brothers and sisters. This is our goal. The only place we can begin, however, is where we now are. We are a people who are unrighteous. God's kingdom cannot come to a people who are unrighteous. We cannot be a God-fearing nation in name only; it must be in deed. We can, with Habakkuk climb the ladder of faith and pray, "O Lord, revive thy work," and then live so God can answer the prayer through us.

May there come a new dedication that shall capture us, this nation, and ultimately the world. It will happen if there is in us a renewed conviction concerning the place of God and the priority of his eternal kingdom. It will happen if there is a real consecration and we commit our-we might go further in our striving toward a world of peace. It will happen if there is a depth of compassion so that, like Christ who wept over Jerusalem, people will know that we, too, have a tear in the heart and are eager to share in the ministry of his loving concern.

Hungers of the Human Heart

Chapter 4
The Roots of Religion

"Out of the depths I cry to thee, O Lord!" Ps. 130:01

The Christian religion is man's response to God's initiative in Christ Jesus our Lord. This is important to remember when we think about the roots of religion. Religion is no invention of man, no self-planned scheme by which he might discover the meaning and purpose for life. Essentially and initially it is God's action, not man's. Even when man thinks he is seeking God, he is but responding to the God who has first sought him in Christ, the seeking Savior. It is God's initiative in love. It is man's response in love. God willingly sent his only Son to bear the cross. It is man's responsibility to take up that cross and follow him. The Bible records God's activity in reaching fallen man. The creation story reminds us that man was created in the image of God. He was meant to be good, to live by the motive of love. Just as God is love, so we by nature if we are true to our calling, are children of love.

In the Old Testament, God spoke through his chosen prophets. These men of God with moral and righteous judgment would listen to and speak for him. They made relevant the justice and mercy of the Almighty One to the needs of sinful man. The New Testament is the continuation of the magnificent story of God's initiative and love.

Hungers of the Human Heart

He sent his Son to redeem us. Jesus came to seek and to save. "For God so loved the world that he gave his only Son, that whoever believes in him should not perish but have eternal life. For God sent the Son into the world, not to condemn the world, but that the world might be saved through him." (John 3:16-17.) The roots of the Christian religion begin with the heavenly Fa-ther and his initiative in Christ and our response to that initiative.

Man Wants to Know the Purpose of Life

From the human element, how did we get started in our religious activity? There is a "rootage" in man — a deep yearning for knowledge. Man wants to know. He is eager to understand the purpose and destiny of life. Man wants to know what is in store eternally, not just tomorrow. Aristotle summed it well when he said, "All men desire by nature to know." The whole curious instinct and desire for knowledge is God planted and God given. Religion is that activity on man's part to discover and know for himself the purpose of life.

Man desires first to know the "self" that God would have him to be. To this self he must be true if he would understand the joys of the abundant life. At the innermost center of his being the created one is hungry for the truth that comes from understanding, as best he can, his nature and destiny, and the nature of his Creator. Man at heart, through his natural desire, is religious. We are told that the word "religion" comes from "religio", meaning "to be or to bind together." Somehow there is a yearning deep within to put it all together, to understand and know the purpose of life. The questions which haunt us must be answered. The psalmist proclaimed,

The fear of the Lord is the beginning of wisdom;
a good understanding have all those who practice it.
-Ps. 111:10

Fear in this connection means the love, the adoration, the proper

38

respect for God. When we love God rightly we gain in wisdom.

Approximately thirty years following the death and resur-rection of Jesus, we find another who wrote some very helpful words to all who are interested in real knowledge. In a prison in Rome, Paul, the greatest apostle who ever lived, was confined. He be-lieved that all things work together for good if we love God. He used his imprisonment as an opportunity to keep close to his Father and close to his brethren in Christ, praying for them and sending messages of love and assurance. While in prison, Paul received news of the Christians in Collossae. They were having difficulty. There was much disorder. They did not understand the centrality of Christ. False teachers and pseudo-wisemen added to the confusion by teaching half truths.

Paul was never in Colossae as far as we know. He did not establish the church, nevertheless he felt a close kinship with all churches and all Christians. As a father would sit down and write to his son, he wrote these words to the Christians in Colossae: "Christ himself! For it is in him, and in him alone, that men will find all the treasures of wisdom and knowledge." (Col. 2:3 Phillips) Christ re-veals the absolute truth of God. Christ is the truth" He said of him-self, "I am the way, the truth, and the life." (John 14:6) The Bible, this beautiful Word of God, tells us in so many places, that His is the way of love. When addressing some early followers, Jesus said, "If you continue in my word, you are truly my disciples, and you will know the truth and the truth will make you free." (John 8:31-32) Knowing this brings joy to the individuals.

We bow humbly in the presence of truth, then stand tall to appropriate its power as we move out to affirm life, saying a hearty "yes" to all that is beautiful and good. We can worship and adore God, glorify Him and enjoy Him forever. We serve Him by minis-tering to others in his name. And, as we do we keep learning more of the purpose of life. It is an exciting and rewarding pilgrimage!

Man Wants to Be

Another "rootage" of religion on man's part is that we want

to be the best person we are capable of becoming. Man is eager to know that his life is counting; he wants to amount to something. He desires to discover a purpose for living, to do something that is lasting to contribute in time that which will outlast time. Life must be more than just day after day of meaningless or secondary activity.

Man wants to be who he is meant to be and do what he was meant to do. His heart is hungry for achievement. If man is to do good, he must first be good. This is the weakness of so many "do-gooders" who join clubs and lodges and get into all types of activities to build a new world. Man will never build a new world apart from God. He would not know how to do it. Without God he will never receive the power to do what he knows he ought to do.

The time has come to do more serious thinking about the moral law. H. Richard Niebuhr has characterized the prevailing American religion in frighteningly clear words. "We believe in a God without wrath who brings men without sin into a heaven without judgment." You can be a good moral person without being a Christian, but you cannot be a Christian without being a good moral person. The quality of our morality is determinative of the real person within. Furthermore we still get out of life what we put into it. A carpenter was approached by one who said, "I have saved enough money to build a lovely home. Put the best of materials in it. You see, this is to be a home for a very special friend of mine. I plan to give it to him. Do your best." But the man build with inferior materials. He used much poor wood, covering it over with good wood on the outside where it would be seen. The time came when the house was finished. The owner came and was presented with the key. Imagine the surprise of the builder when the gentleman handed the key back to him saying, "Keep the keys. For years I have been wanting to do something for you. I thought the best I could do would be to have you build a house for yourself. It's all yours!"

Teddy Roosevelt said it aptly. "To educate the mind without educating the morals is to educate a menace to society." Man is basically restless until he finds moral responsibility to which he can give himself. This is always related to his inner happiness and to the destiny of his soul. Margaret Blair Johnstone tells of an incident at a meeting she attended.

For the next hour or so the conversation was a brickbat-throwing match regarding religion, morals, sex, and intellectual hypocrisy. Through it all, I said little. As it turned out, it was best I did. For finally, one of the radio editors said, "You know, this party reminds me of another I once attended. There was a girl named Mary, a well known character you'd all agree: Well, we were all sitting around that night swapping dirty stories. We were not discussing religion, believe me! But one guy knew Mary was hipped on religion,so he decided he'd have some fun. 'What's the most important thing in the world?' he asked. Then he gave his answer: 'I think it's finding a willing blonde.' The rest of us all took the ball and really passed it. There's no point going into details, but everybody tossed in his own smut...that is, all except Mary. Finally, the fellow who asked the question put Mary on the spot. 'Why so quiet, Mary? You've got no right taking all and adding nothing. Come on, give! What's the most important thing in the world?"

"I was just waiting," said Mary. "I wanted to see what the rest of you thought."

"Well—?" "There is only one really important thing," Mary said. "It's the chance given us here and now to save our souls for all eternity"[1]

Man is on his way to real becoming when he confesses his sin and accepts the forgiving mercy of the loving Father. This will very naturally lead him to live the good life. It is quite a humbling observation to see the brilliant intelligence of man; and yet, with all his accomplishments, man has not learned how to live in peace with his brothers. With all that man knows, with more high school diplomas and more college degrees, still crime and violence are prevalent. Perhaps we need to say it again and again: To educate the mind without educating the morals, is to educate a menace to society. Before man can ever find eternal significance he must have a driving desire to make his life count for something. He must begin by being good in order that he can do good. This driving desire is part of the rootage of religion. It is man's attempt to find and follow a God who is worth finding and following.

Man Wants Help

Another rootage of religion is that man knows he must have help. When man begins to understand and know himself he sees himself as a lost sheep who has gone astray. He knows himself to be a sinner. He is separated not only from God and a proper relationship with his fellow man but separated from his own best self.

The Bible makes clear the cost of this separation. It means spiritual disease and death. But thank God the Bible also makes clear our way of deliverance! Katherine Mansfield, a British writer, spent most of her childhood in New Zealand. She died of tuberculosis at the age of thirty-four. While in the sanatorium, she wrote, "Since I came here, I have been very interested in the Bible. I have read the Bible for hours on end." She lamented that she had not learned sooner what the Bible contained. "Facts like these," she said, "ought to have been part of my breathing." She had a right to know the vivid stories of the Old Testament and the vital stories of the New Testament. Said Paul of Timothy's home: "From a child thou hast known the holy scriptures, which are able to make thee wise unto salvation through faith which is in Christ Jesus," (II Tim. 3:15 K.J.V.) If the Bible can make us wise unto salvation, then we had better turn to the Bible, learn what it means to be saved and find therein how to be saved.

The magnificent one hundred and thirtieth psalm could have been written by any of us. It is a plea for God's forgiving grace. The man who wrote it acknowledged that he was a sinner in need of God's mercy. Each one of us can profit from it.

" Out of the depths I cry to thee, O Lord!

[1]Margaret Blair Johnstone, When God Says No: Faith's Starting Point (New York: Simon & Schuster, Inc. 1954) Used by permission.

Lord, hear my voice!
Let thy ears be attentive
to the voice of my supplications!

If thou, O Lord, shouldst mark iniquities,
Lord, who could stand?
But there is forgiveness with thee,
 that thou mayest be feared.

I wait for the Lord, my soul waits,
and in his word I hope;
my soul waits for the Lord
more than watchmen for the morning,
more than watchmen for the morning.

O Israel, hope in the Lord!
For with the Lord there is steadfast love,
and with him is plenteous redemption.
And he will redeem Israel from all his iniquities.

Man must be religious. He must have God's saving help to redeem him. God's grace is his love and mercy in action. Without this man would be most miserable. "Since all have sinned and fall short of the glory of God, they are justified by his grace as a gift, through the redemption which is in Christ Jesus." (Rom. 3:23-24.) Here it is! Man is saved by the free gift of God's grace. He need not fret because he cannot possibly earn his salvation. All he must do is receive it. "For by grace you have been saved through faith; and this is not your own doing, it is the gift of God." (Eph. 2:8.)

This is the word of assurance bringing peace to our souls. Man's sins can be forgiven. Man's soul can be in right relationship with God. Man can be a new creature in Christ. This is the purpose of religion, not to speak pious platitudes, but to get down to business so that man knows his sins are forgiven by a God whose love is perfect. Man wants to know. Man wants to be. And man knows he must have the help that only God can give.

Man Wants to Help

Another rootage of religion on man's part is that he wants to help. Man was meant to help his brother. It is part of the nature of creation. Man, if he is true to his own calling, wants to be a helper, a part of God's redemptive fellowship for the salvation of all people. The call to heroic witness and service is ever a part of his being.

When Handel was writing his great Messiah he wept as he worked on the phrase "he was despised and rejected of men." For once he saw the true meaning of the cross as he had never seen it before. Jesus, the perfect one, was nailed to a cross. Out of the creative anguish of his soul Handel wrote The Messiah. Man must interpret the meaning of the cross to the generation in which he is privileged to live. We cannot be religious or find our mission in life until we find that which causes us to give of our strength to the meeting of the problems of the world. We must interpret the meaning of the cross to those in need.

Some years ago, before the days of blood banks, a little girl lay desperately ill. The only thing that could save her was a transfusion. They found that her thirteen-year-old brother, Jimmy, had just the right type of blood. The doctor asked Jimmy if he would give his blood, and he answered, "Yes, sir, if she needs it." Jimmy lay down on a bed beside that of his sister. They put the needle in his arm. After a few minutes Jimmy looked up at the doctor and asked, "When am I going to die?" He thought he would have to die to save his sister's life; yet he did not hesitate. Do you realize that there is a hero in your soul like the hero in Jimmy's soul? Don't crush that hero! Let him rise to fulfillment and maturity. This is part of the function of religion.

What a wonderful thing it is to know that there is a God who is calling us to help meet the needs of others! We can all say, "If Christ died for me, I will live for him." It was in the month of May, 1863, when President Abraham Lincoln was visiting in a ward where there were men who had been wounded in battle. He came to one young fellow just sixteen years of age, a lad from Vermont, who was obviously fatally wounded. Big old Abe Lincoln went up and took the boy by the hand and said, "Well, my son, what can I do for you?" The boy replied, "Will you write a letter to my mother?" So the President sat down in a chair. He asked for writing materials. As the boy dictated, the President wrote a very long letter. He assured the boy that as soon as he got back to his office it would be sent to his mother. And then he asked, "Is there anything else I can do for you?" The youth said, "Won't you just stay with me a little longer? I'd like to hold your hand." The President remained, waiting for over two hours, until the boy passed on to his heavenly home. Mr. Lincoln then took the boy's hands and laid them across his chest and quietly slipped out of the hospital with tears streaming down his cheeks.

Here is greatness because it is love in action. Everyone of us can go out of our way to do good unto others. This doing of good in the spirit of Christ is a part of the role of the religious life. And furthermore we are blest in the process. We can rejoice and give thanks for the unfinished tasks which await us. Our participation in the ministry of love pleases God, blesses others, and enriches our own lives.

> Creation's Lord, we give Thee thanks
> That this Thy world is incomplete;
> That battle calls our marshaled ranks,
> That work awaits our hands and feet;
>
> That Thou hast not yet finished man,
> That we are in the making still,
> As friends who share the Maker's plan,
> As sons who know the Father's will.
>
> Beyond the present sin and shame,

Wrong's bitter, cruel, scorching blight,
We see the beckoning vision flame,
The blessed kingdom of the right.

What though the Kingdom long delay,
And still with haughty foes must cope?
It gives us that for which to pray,
 A friend for toil and faith and hope.

Since what we choose is what we are,
And what we love we yet shall be,
The goal may ever shine afar;
The will to win it makes us free.[2]

I have a wealthy friend whose life has taken on a new radiance and joy since he learned how to share his financial resources to help others. Ours is the choice. We are free to choose the extent to which we will help alleviate the suffering hurts of others. But let us make no mistake about it — we do ourselves a favor when we share what we are and what we have to help others. Love is not just something we feel or think; love is what we do!

My friend Bishop Ernest T. Dixon, Jr. tells of a young man who was alone with his fiancee. He sat in silence for a period of time. Finally, his fiancee, attempted to create conversation, inquired, "John, tonight what would you rather be than anything else in the world?"

John thought a moment, then said, "A big octopus."

"Why an octopus?" she asked.

"So I could take all my twenty-five arms and wrap them around you real tight," was his answer.

"Go on, John," she said; "you aren't doing anything with the two arms you have."

To the degree that we love we will use what we are and what we have to help others and build the kind of a world where all

[2]"Creation's Lord, we Give Thee Thanks," by William De Witt Hyde.

people can enjoy life fully. The late, great Walter Ranschenbusch used to say that we "never live so intensely as when we love strongly." Then he would add, "We never realize ourselves so vividly as when we are in the full glow of love for for others." To love is to live. And love is never lost. Even if not reciprocated, as Washington Irving reminds us, "it will flow back and soften and purify the heart."

At best, the roots of religion begin in God Religion is man's response to God's initiative in Christ Jesus our Lord, who was willing to suffer death upon the cross that we might be saved. There is also a rootage of religion because man wants to know the purpose of life. He wants to really amount to something, to contribute to this life that which will go beyond, to find eternal destiny and significance for his living. Man wants help. He must be saved from his sins, so he cried unto the Lord who is faithful, just, and eager to forgive. Freed from his own captive self, man wants to meet the needs of others and give his life that they might be saved. This is life's great mission. May He grant that we shall rise up and meet the challenge to be what God meant for us to be when he blessed us with the gift of life and love.

Hungers of the Human Heart

Chapter 5
How Can I Know God?

"The fool says in his heart, 'There is no God.'" --Psalms 14:1

Many of us sometime in life ask the basic question, "Does God exist?" We may not be so foolish as to declare there is no God, but we have honest doubts. We wonder. Does he really exist? If there is a God why is he so distant from me? We, like Job of old, with all his troubles, trials, and tribulations, also cry out, "Oh, that I knew where I might find Him." (Job 23:3).

Let me suggest that there are two ways that we can know God. The first is from an honest study of the written Word, the Bible. The second is from our own personal experience.

In all of this the important thing is to be honest with ourselves. Do I really want to know God? Norman Vincent Peale says we should beware of our "cherished desires." He adds, "We tend to get that which we desire with our whole heart." In the Old Testament, in the book of Deuteronomy we read, "Seek the Lord your God, and you will find him if you search after him with all your heart and with all your soul." (Deut. 4:29.) In the New Testament we find Jesus speaking and saying, "Ask and it will be given you; seek and you will find; knock, and it will be opened to you. For everyone who asks receives, and he who seeks finds, and to him who knocks it will be opened." (Matt. 7:7-8)

Hungers of the Human Heart

To discover truth in the field of religion is not unlike that in any other area of learning. An honest and open, humble and eager inquiry is obviously necessary. Zephaniah issues an invitation, "Come together and hold assembly...seek the Lord, all you humble of the land, who do his commands; seek righteousness, seek humility..." (Zeph. 2:1-3).

We begin acknowledging that we know we do not know it all but that there is more to be learned if we seek truth with the whole heart and mind and are really humble and open to that which is to be revealed. The writer of Hebrews says, "... whoever would draw near to God must believe that he exists and that he rewards those who seek him. (Heb. 11:14-16.)

It is important to be fair to oneself in seeking the truth of God. The only place we can begin is where we now are. It is to no avail to bewail our ignorance or lack of adequate knowledge. Even the pursuit of the truth of God is an exciting adventure. So let's be fair with ourselves as we join in the quest for the knowledge of God's existence and availability to bless his children. This is a far better approach than to belittle ourselves for what we have not yet discovered.

A preacher entered a Sunday School class while the lesson was in progress and asked the children some questions. "Who broke down the walls of Jericho?" A boy answered, "Not me, sir." The preacher turned to the teacher and asked, "Is this the usual standard in this class?" The teacher answered, "This boy is honest and I believe him. I really don't think he did it." Leaving the room in disgust, the preacher sought out the deacon in charge of teaching and explained what had happened. The deacon said, "I have known both the teacher and the boy for some time, and neither of them would do such a thing." By this time the preacher was heartsick and reported it to the deacons. They said, "We see no point in being disturbed. Let's turn the bill for the damage to the walls over to the Finance Committee and charge it to upkeep."

In the Kansas home of former United States President Dwight Eisenhower, the Bible was read daily. His well-thumbed

Bible had the words of Genesis 1 underscored, "In the beginning God." General Eisenhower said, "That's where our nation started and that's where my parents and forefathers started." Mr. Eisenhower added, "The Bible is endorsed by the ages. Our civilization is built on its words. In no other book is there such a collection of inspired wisdom, reality and hope. It describes the condition of man and the promise of man with such power that, through many eras and generations, it has made the mighty humble and has strengthened the weak."

Although I am no scientist, the longer I live the more it seems to me that there is no basic conflict between science and faith. Many of us find ourselves in agreement with Dr. William Pollard, the atomic scientist who speaks of the "twin mysteries," meaning science and faith. In March, 1972, I heard him speak at Scarritt College in Nashville, Tennessee. In this message he said, "The deeper one probes into the make-up of matter, into the eons of space and time, or into the intricate, infinitesimal complications of living things , the more mysterious it all becomes and the closer we are drawn to the ultimate mystery." Dr. Pollard related ultimate mystery to the "transcendent" reference both in Israel and in Jesus Christ. He believes there is much strong evidence in this present century that we are going to recover the reality of the transcendent. He concluded, "It is hard for me to imagine anyone hearing of creation and the activity of the known universe, not to believe in a transcendent purposeful creator - God."

From the beginning of the Bible to the end we can learn of God's activity, in creation and in the hearts and minds of those whom he has created. Once we experience his great word of love as revealed in the one who came to make known the existence of God's love for us, we become "new creatures in Christ." Nothing takes the place of our own seeking and of our own experience.

In any discussion of religion, in any attempt to find and know God, there are basically two approaches. You can begin with theology which is our forefathers' attempt to explain the meaning of their religious experiences. But theology alone will not suffice. At best it is the road map pointing the way. We experience the true joy of the journey only when we take the trip for ourselves. When asked to define New Orleans jazz, Louis Armstrong said, "Man, when you got to ask what it is, you'll never get to know." A real religion must be an experienced religion. Man can never understand what it means to be saved until he has experienced the joy of salvation. Another approach to religion and life is to begin with man, where he is in his relationship to other men and as he knows the oughtness of life. If we are systematic in our quest for moral understanding, we will soon know that there is a God. Either the deductive or the inductive approach will bring one to the same place. God as the sovereign Being must be acknowledged if man is to become that for which he was intended and for which he desires.

Tolstoy once said, "God is without whom we cannot live." After many years of experience with people in and out of the church Bishop Gerald Kennedy said, "I never met an atheist. I have met a few people who claimed they were atheists but when we talked it over, it always seemed to me they were objecting to someone else's idea of God rather than insisting that there was no God."

The father of our country, and its first president, George Washington said, "It is impossible to reason without arriving at a Supreme Being." As far back as 1770 Voltaire stated that, "If God did not exist, it would be necessary to invent him." Men must worship something or someone. It is interesting to note that the word "atheism" is not used in the Bible. It is assumed that we will worship. The main concern of the authors of the Bible is that men will worship something less than God. Idolatry has always been a prevailing sin and yet from the time of Moses to the end of the Book we are told:

> "I am the Lord thy God and thou shalt have no
> other gods before me. Thou shalt not make unto
> me any graven images." (Ex.20:2-3.)

A study of the Bible will help one to understand the activity of God through history. It records the mighty acts of a loving father.

He is more than a cosmic force, and more than supreme intelligence. He is the creator. We are his creatures. He is the Father, we are his children. He is Lord of history and if we choose to allow him, he can be Lord of our lives.

Most of us are interested in a good education for ourselves and our children. In his book, "Human Nature in the Bible", William Lyon Phelps wrote, "I thoroughly believe in a university education for both men and women but I believe a knowledge of the Bible without a college course is more valuable than a college course without the Bible."

In 1965 it was my privilege to serve as pastor of Central Methodist Church of Phoenix, Arizona when Vonda Kay Van Dyke won the Miss America contest. Many of us will remember the tear-dimmed eyes when we joined with millions who were blessed with her sincere and humble witness of her faith that night. In October of that year she joined in our Layman's Day Service and said, "My Bible is the most important book I own. The Bible has something more than words on pages. Its thoughts have transforming power. It was through the Scriptures that I found new life in Christ. By daily reading its message, I can find assurance, strength, faith, and guidance for the road ahead. The Bible is the Book of Life to me."

When we read the Bible we remember the words of James who said, "God opposes the proud, but gives grace to the humble. . .draw near to God and he will draw near to you. . . humble yourself before the Lord and he will exalt you." (James 4:6-10.) Although we read the Bible with a humility of spirit and an open mind, we will never completely understand everything. It will be well to recall what Mark Twain used to say in this regard, "Most people are bothered by those passages in scripture which they cannot understand. But as for me, I have always noticed that the passages that troubled me the most are those which I do understand."

The book of Genesis tells of the creation and of God's evaluation of his handiwork. Over and over again he declared it "good." He created male and female in his own image and assumed that we too were "good." God was pleased. He wants us all to refrain from

53

sinful negativism and from the hurts we impose on others and ourselves so that we might enjoy this good land of ours and our relationships with one another. The Psalmist declared, "I believe that I shall see the goodness of the Lord in the land of the living! (Ps. 27:13.) What a privilege it is to expect, look for, and experience the goodness of God in living relationships of love! There is nothing like it. There is a bumper sticker some people put on their cars which reads: "P. S. 'I love you.' Jesus." Let's do ourselves a favor and remember that the message of love is no simple P. S., it is the whole story of God which experience has revealed in the Christ of the New Testament. The young disciple, John as a mature man, looking back over his life and his experience with the Man of Galilee opened his account of the life of Jesus with these words:

> "In the beginning was the Word, and the Word was
> with God, and the Word was God. He was in the
> beginning with God; all things were made through
> him, and without him was not anything made that
> was made. In him was life, and the life was the light
> of men. The light shines in the darkness, and the dark-
> ness has not overcome it." (John 1:1-5.)

John also indicated that to as many as received him, and who believed in his name he gave power to become children of God. John added that this Word of God "became flesh and dwelt among us, full of grace and truth; we have beheld his glory, glory as of the only Son of the Father. (John 1:14) It is a great thing to believe in the one who is the Word, and the Light. Most of us have had experiences with children who feared the dark. It seems as though when we are adults we fear the light even more. We sometimes shy away from the light that can show us the way to life abundant and eternal. I am not impressed when told to place my hand in the hand of God and walk out into the darkness. The walk of faith is the journey of love with the One who said, "I am the light of the world; he who follows me will not walk in darkness, but will have the light of life." (John 8:12.) To follow the God of truth with the Master of love is to walk in the light of a known way. It has been tried and tested by millions and proven to be true. Faith is no blind leap into the abyss of darkness. It is the way of light and life!

To discover, from our study of the written word, that "God is love," is to discover that which frees us to really live. Many of us are familiar with the story of the Prodigal Son, as recorded in Luke chapter 15. We all can relate to him. At times we have been much like him. And yet this is not so much the story about the son as it is the nature of the loving father waiting for his own to return home. The same can be said of John 14, often referred to as the "Mansion Chapter," because it speaks of the resurrection and the life eternal. But again, this does not deal so much with the idea of a mansion or heavenly home, though it does this, as to remind us again of the nature of God. The word "Mansion" or "House" is used but once. The word "Father" appears 23 times in this single chapter. We have a father who cares! He wants to see us all redeemed for all time and eternity.

His word of love as revealed in the Bible has withstood its critics. It stands.

The Anvil — God's Word

Last eve I passed beside a blacksmith's door,
And heard the anvil ring the vesper chime;
Then looking in, I saw upon the floor
Old hammers, worn with beating years of time.

"How many anvils have you had," said I,
"To wear and batter all these hammers so?"
"Just one," said he, and then, with twinkling eye,
"The anvil wears the hammers out, you know."

And so, thought I, the anvil of God's Word,
For ages skeptic blows have beat upon;
Yet, though the noise of falling blows was heard,
The anvil is unharmed — the hammers gone.

— Author Unknown

Hungers of the Human Heart

From Communist Russia, with its emphasis on atheistic materialism, has come quite a number of persons who still attest to their Christian faith. Many of us recall with gladness the words of Mr. Stalin's daughter Svetlana, who said it clearly and forcefully, "You simply cannot live without God."

My friend, Dr. Frank Williams was one who visited behind the Iron Curtain in Russia in the summer of 1963. They spent seventeen days with a very intelligent young lady guide. She told them at the outset that She did not believe in God, that she was an atheist. At the end of the seventeen day period they gave her a gift and sang, "Let me call you sweetheart." She wiped a few tears from her eyes and said, "I do not believe in God, but I have watched you people, your witness, and listened to your singing. I have enjoyed your fellowship, so very much. If it is your faith in God that makes you like you are, I want it."

Personal Experience

Karl Barth will always be remembered as one of the greatest theologians of the twentieth century. When he was asked to name the most important single Christian truth, he is reported to have said, "Jesus loves me, this I know, for the Bible tells me so." Imagine, such a learned scholar, speaking such a simple yet profound truth! He found it in the written word and from his own personal experience.

When we love it is our response to the love of God. We are told that "He first loved us." To experience this wonderful love of God is to desire to share it with others. As the late Roy A. Burkhart used to say, "Love, after all, is the response of the divine in one person to the divine in another, and it is the response of one's true nature to the Father." Dr. Burkhart believed this and lived this. Many of us were blessed of God just to come in contact with His warm and loving personality. This author has had the same thing happen to him in such a rewarding experience when spending a week with Dr. Albert Schweitzer. With his accent on his philosophy of "reverence for life" he reminded us that "no human being is ever totally or permanently a stranger to another human being." He was right. Man belongs to man. Just as the wave does not exist for itself, but is a part of the ocean so each individual is a part of humanity. We belong to

one another and together we belong to God and, thank God, He cares! The song, "No one Ever Cared for Me Like Jesus" touches and blesses us because Jesus, the Son of God, revealed to us the true nature of the Father. Ralph W. Sockman told the Chicago Sunday Evening Club of how a lawyer had as a child experienced this closeness of God to himself. "My religious faith can be expressed in a boyhood experience. I was taken by my father to New York City. I was little, and to keep from getting lost I clung to his finger, but after a while in the crowds and the long steps, I grew tired, and my fingers began to slip, I looked up to him and said, 'Father, you'll have to take hold of my hand now. I can't hold on much longer.'" And we can all imagine, can't we, how his father's hand grasped the little hand of his son and helped him through the crowds? How true of life!

Not only little boys but also grown men and women find their lives enriched when they experience the security of the love of God. Marconi, inventor of the wireless, was sitting with a friend on the coast of New- foundland waiting all night for the signal which would indicate the success of his labors. When it finally came Marconi was like a man caught up in the clouds. He said, "That proves I have not been off on a crazy whim of my own but that there is at the center of the someone who is holding my hand."

Whatever our experiences of life may be, whether they be sad or glad, hurtful or helpful, if we are open and responsive, we can know from our own personal experience that God's love is available to see us through. The Reverend Stanley Brown was once a member of the church I served in Chicago. After saying, "yes" to the call of God to become a preacher, he later spent five years on the ministerial staff of Central Methodist Church of Phoenix, Arizona. He enjoys sharing an experience of many years ago. He puts it this way, "When I was a very young child I was badly burned. Some refuse was burning in the alley and I was poking around in it. A five gallon can of oil was in there. It exploded and covered me with fire. My father raced to snatch me up in his arms, smothering the fire. He ran with me to the house where they treated the burns on my legs. It's a strange thing, but as I recall that experience I cannot remember the pain or how it felt. Yet no sooner do I recall that day to mind than I remember, so well, my father's arms." I remember them around me; I remember in the midst of the flames that assurance that all would be well because I was in my father's arms. When you enter your Gethsemane, and fight the painful battle with yourself, the one thing that will win the day is to trust in the Father's arms. Like Jesus in prayer, surrender it all to the Father and He will strengthen you

All of us at times are lonely and insecure. We want to know that someone really cares. This is where a thorough study of the scripture comes in so handy. We are enriched when we read, for example, I Corinthians 13 and find the Apostle Paul, concluding, "so faith, hope, love abide these three; but the greatest of these is love." (I Cor. 13:13) It must be pointed out, that God is not faith, nor is He hope. God is love! And love is that which can only be experienced in the present. It doesn't mean much to say to someone, "I used to love you," or again, "someday I may learn to love you." Unless it is real today it cannot be experienced. To know that God loves us now and that others care for us now blesses and fills the emptiness of our loneliness.

A number of years ago newspapers in America told of a Chinese student who had lived a number of years in the attic of a church in Michigan. With high hopes he had left home, enrolled at the university, but flunked out. He thought this would mean disgrace for his parents. He couldn't face them or anyone, so he hid. At night he would go down to the church kitchen and eat leftovers from the church luncheons and suppers. He got clothing from the rummage bags. Needless to say, he was terribly lonely! Sundays were special days for him. He would crawl down and hide behind the choir loft where he could be as close to the choir members as possible without being seen. The only thing that separated him from the choir members was a thin wall. He longed to reach out and touch the people, but couldn't. Of course, he was finally discovered. When his story became known it was spread by the newspapers throughout the land. The most encouraging thing was the fact that the local congregation took that young lad into their hearts and let him know that they really cared. He no longer lived in the attic alone. He was a part of their church family fellowship. One wonders how many lonely and burdened people there are in the world who long to reach out in an effort to clasp a helping hand. Insecurity and fear of rejection keeps them from really making known the depth of their despair. The Negro spiritual, "Nobody Knows the Trouble I've Seen," no doubt speaks to the experience in the lives of most of us.

We will never agree on church doctrines. They are manmade and subject to error. We chuckle when reminded of Carl Sandburg who once said, "I only made one grammatical mistake in my life, but the moment I done it I seen it." Is it not time to admit that we have made mistakes in trying to become unified as a worldwide family of God around doctrine? It is love that frees us and unites us. The love of God which we know and bondage of the past to be truly human and truly spiritual. It also has within it the power to unite us. Of necessity, we agree to disagree on certain doctrines, but resolve to be united in His love. None of us can make it alone. We need one another and we need God.

The noted pianist Van Cliburn was asked in an interview, "What directs your life?" Cliburn answered, "The power of God that governs everything. The presence of the living Christ. I try to face life with what I call the Christ-consciousness." And then he made this observation: "Frankly, I don't see how people can live in twentieth-century society amid all its besetting problems without God."

If you, my reader, are a struggling inquirer, seeking for the truth of God, you may well ask ! "but how can I know all of this for myself?" This is a basic question. It is one that haunts modern man.

Hungers of the Human Heart

This matter of espistemology is always a major need. How can I learn? How can I know? There are three major ways. We deal with our religious quest the same as in any other area of knowledge. First of all we can learn from Sense Perception. The five senses have much to teach us. Just "stop, look and listen" for a while, to behold the beauty of God in His world, is to learn much. In so doing we too may say "The heavens declare the glory of God and the firmament shows his handiwork."

> "When I look at thy heavens, the work of thy fingers,
> the moon and the stars which thou hast established;
> what is man that thou art mindful of him,
> and the son of man that thou dost care for him?
> Yet thou hast made him little less than God,
> and dost crown him with glory and honor. . .
> O Lord, our Lord,
> how majestic is thy name in all the earth! (Psalms 8:3-94)

If ravens were to bring our food to the front door each day or if bread would fall from the sky in our yard each day, we would declare this a miracle. But is it no less a miracle that we can plant a seed in the ground, see it sprout and grow, and with sunshine and rain, develop into a mature plant and provide food? It is all a miracle of God's grace and providential care. The Irish poet, Thomas Moore ! over 100 years ago spoke of some of this;

> The Glory of God in Creation
> Thou art, O God, the life and light
> Of all this wondrous world we see;
> Its glow by day, its smile by night,
> Are hut reflections caught from Thee.
> Where'er we turn, Thy glories shine,
> And all things fair and bright are Thine!

A second way to gain knowledge is through Rational Judg-

60

ment. It may be that you remember, as I do, having a father who used to say with emphasis, "Use your noodle!" This admonition usually followed a real and obvious faux pas. In the field of religion as in any other field of endeavor it is necessary to remember that we do have minds, which is as many have stated "the greatest computer ever made."

Faith and reason compliment one another. Faith will at times go beyond reason, but it is not unreasonable. A study of the past experiences and deeds of men and women of faith through the centuries will provide plenty of documentation to the reasonableness of faith.

Still a third way, in this business of epistomology by which we learn is through Intuitive Insight. It behooves us to follow our hunches, especially if we know people will be helped in doing so. This could well be the voice of God directing us. Any meaningful religious experience will have a touch of the mystical in it. Intuitively we sometimes know what to do. Mysticism in religion is one way we can discover God within ourselves. We can experience a union with Him.

I remember attending a university homecoming when a friend spoke to me about her surprise that I had ended up in the ministry. She had the audacity to declare "I never thought you would become a preacher!" She then wished me well, but said that she had never had a religious experience. I asked her if she had any children. She said, "Oh, yes, we have three beautiful daughters!" t I then said, "You have given birth to three beautiful daughters and you say you have never had a religious experience! You have had religious experiences all right, you just haven't called them that."

This could well be said of many people. Sense perception, ration- al judgment and intuitive insight, working together can reveal so much of God's truth for man.

The wonderful thing about God is that he is not totally other. It is true, he is transcendent but he is also imminent. He is near. Jesus said he was within. When the son of God came they called him

Immanuel, meaning "God with us." As a grown man this Jesus said, "He who has seen me has seen the Father." (John 14:9.) Those who followed Him kept asking,"What must we do to be doing the work of God? Jesus answered them, "This is the work of God that you believe in Him whom he has sent." (John 6:28-30.) To know God through personal experience is, not so much the result of doing the good deeds he wants us to do in His name, though this we will do, it is to really believe in Him. We may not be quite as legalistic as the Jews in Jesus day, but we still have our hang-ups on good deeds. The Gospel tells us of the free gift of His grace. A gift can never be earned. It can only be received.

The Apostle Paul, who wrote so much to make plain that "it is by grace that you are saved through faith" said, "If you confess with your lips that Jesus is Lord and believe in your heart that God raised him from the dead, you will be saved. For man believes with his heart and is justified and he confesses with his lips and so is saved." (Romans 10:9-10.)

False Solutions

During his first year in office as Mayor of Los Angeles Tom Bradley visited First United Methodist Church of North Hollywood. He sat on a piano bench with this pastor and talked especially to the children and young people. Realizing the danger of drugs he advised, "Get high on Jesus." All of us have a desire to be turned on, to really be alive and gloriously aware. We pursue life and this is good. And yet, there are so many times when we seek false solutions for the living of life and our turn-ons.

In one city where I pastored we had three young men caught and jailed as vandals. One of these young fellows was from a church family in our parish. The boys had had their fill of beer, stole a car and drove up and down the neighborhood with ball bats smashing headlights and windshields on several dozen or more automobiles. The judge asked, "Why did you do it?" One of them replied, "For the thrill of it."

When I went to visit the young man from our church family I shook his hand and said, "Congratulations" He looked at me as though I was out of my mind. I told him that I was proud that he wanted to get a thrill out of life, that this was my desire too. Naturally we did discuss the fact that his methodology had led to a short range thrill with some pretty serious consequences. I did point out to the lad that there is one who said, "I came that you may have life and have it abundantly." (John 10:10.) This same Jesus said, "Abide in me . . .as the branch cannot bear fruit by itself, unless it abides in the vine, neither can you, unless you abide in me. I am the vine, you are the branches . . . apart from me you can do nothing . . . these things I have spoken to you, that my joy may be in you, and that your joy may be full." (John 15:4-11.)

It is good to report that the young men, while on probation, made restitution for all damages. A year later the young man from our parish, after having become very active in church life, was elected an officer of the young people's organization. He decided he would not settle for a shallow fun experience when he could have joy.

It is estimated that in the United States alone each year there are 25,000 deaths from automobile accidents (half the total of traffic deaths) attributed to drivers under the influence of alcohol. It is a killer. It is quite common to be invited to participate in an attitudinal adjustment hour where people are supposedly changed and improved because of the beverage, alcohol. It is understandable to want to seek a release from our problems and to experience the sense of feeling good. It is obvious, that at least for so many, this is a false solution to life's desired goal. 10,000,000 alcoholics, 25,000,000 problem drinkers and 25,000 deaths speak sufficiently of the misuse of alcohol. Alcohol has to be the number one drug problem in the world today.

Since The Free Speech Movement of 1964 we have seen much of the so-called drug culture. Thousands of youths have died since beginning the use of drugs. Many parents understand what Francis Bacon said a number of hundreds of years ago, "The griefs of parents are private."

Hungers of the Human Heart

When asked why use drugs some have replied that they do it "for kicks," "out of curiosity," "to have a mystical experience," "to understand myself better," "as a consciousness expander," and for "religious or philosophical insight." Drugs may give a preliminary experience of mind expansion. The fantasy may be fascinating, the hallucination real but this is the antithesis of the rational process. Drugs pervert and destroy the mind until ones capacity for living a meaningful life is taken away.

This author has spent thousands of hours with drug addicts. Like anyone else it was only natural that they would want to "expand their perceptions," but they became dull. They wanted to experience the joy of living but soon looked tired and sick. More than a few of them died. I believe, with Reuel L. Howe, as he discusses in his book "Survival Plus," that we all have a desire to be sensitive and aware. We want to experience the meaning of the world around us and within us. "Such awareness is not easily achieved or easily maintained." Ours is the privilege of developing an awareness at the door of consciousness so that we can enjoy life fully. This is not only the desire of man, it is the desire of God for man. A turning to the God of scriptures and to the God of Christ is the way to find life. No false solutions are satisfactory.

In 1965, at a national meeting in Miami, Florida we were privileged to hear Gert Behanna, "the late Liz." While there a group of us had a meal together. Gert happened to be talking to another alcoholic, a gentleman from Miami. During the course of their conversation he said,"We alcoholics have no real problem compared to other people. We have learned that we have to turn everything over to God." Gert heartily concurred, in fact this was her main message to the conference.

Taste and See

"Try it, you'11 like it!" How many times have you heard it? I remember calling in the home where a young girl had gotten very active in church. She decided she wanted to declare her faith, confess Christ as her Lord, and be received into the membership of the church. I invited her parents to give serious thought to the same matter. Her father said he wasn't interested. He indicated that he wasn't sure whether he was an atheist or an agnostic. He just didn't believe in God, or anything involving religion. I asked him if he had read the Bible through. He said he hadn't read it at all. I asked, "How in the world can you say you do not believe, when you haven't read the evidence of so many who have believed?" I then challenged him to read from the Bible, particularly the New Testament every day for three months. We also made a deal that he would attend church every Sunday for three months. You can guess the rest. A whole new world opened up to my friend, Jack. He tried it and he liked it. A year later he was superintendent of the high school department of that church. Of course, his daughter was pleased, so was his wife, but most important of all, he had made the discovery for himself.

Many years ago a great leader by the name of David invited his people to "taste and see that the Lord is good!" He had had a great experience with God. Take a look at his own words in the first eight verses of Psalm 34.

"I will bless the Lord at all times; his praise shall continually be in my mouth.
My soul makes its boast in the Lord; let the afflicted hear and be glad.
O magnify the Lord with me, and let us exalt his name together. I sought the Lord, and he answered me, and delivered me from all my fears.
Look to him, and be radiant; so your faces shall never be ashamed This poor man cried, and the Lord heard him, and saved him out of all his troubles.
The angel of the Lord encamps around those who fear him and delivers them.
O taste and see that the Lord is good! Happy is the man who takes refuge in him!" (Psalms 34:1-8.)

Hungers of the Human Heart

Like David of old many of us have cried out unto the Lord and discovered him to be faithful. The Bible shares so much of his eternal goodness. Again David indicates that we need not fret ourselves because of the wicked nor to be envious of wrong-doers. He continues "Trust in the Lord and do good; so you will dwell in the land and enjoy security. Take delight in the Lord, and he will give you the desires of your heart. Commit your way to the Lord; trust in him." (Psalms 37:3-5.)

George Washington Carver was a man with great faith power. Someone asked him,"Why is it that so few people have this power?" "They can," his voice rose to a sweet and almost piercing beauty. "They can, if they only believe." Then he laid his hand on the Bible beside him, the secret lies all in here, right in the promises of God. These promises are real but so few people believe that they are real."

Most of us discover the reality of God and his power when we are hurting. Faith grows in the valley. We enjoy life when things go along smoothly, but we do not learn much. The same is true of an athletic team. Victories are enjoyed but the big lessons are learned when we face defeat and discover how to get ready for the next game. One of our sons pointed out a passage of scripture that had blessed him. It proved to be a blessing to me at a time when I was hurting and needed something extra special. You too may find it helpful. It comes from Isaiah who felt that God was speaking to his children and saying, "Fear not, for I have redeemed you; I have called you by name, you are mine. When you pass through the waters I will be with you; and through the rivers, they shall not overwhelm you; when you] walk through fire you shall not be burned, and the flame shall not consume you. For I am the lord your God, the Holy One of Israel, your Savior. . . Because you are precious in my eyes and honored, and I love you . . . Fear not, for I am with you." (Isa. 43:1-5.)

Just think of the power of these words. We are not to fear, for we have been redeemed, God calls us by name. Our trials and burdens are not overwhelming us because He is with us. And to

66

think we are precious in His eyes and loved. What glorious good news!

A Scottish scholar who had been tortured with doubts and temptations all his life finally was able to say, "When I knew that God loved me, I danced on the Brig o'Dee with delight!" Paul, in writing to the Ephesians reminds us all,that in Christ God has chosen us to be His own. In the famous "I am the vine, ye are the branches" chapter of John at verse 16 Jesus himself says, "You did not choose me, but I chose you."

There is an old hymn that some of us love to sing. The tune is singable and the words are terrific. "At the cross, at the cross where I first saw the light and the burden of my heart rolled away. It was there by faith I received my sight and now I am happy all the day." When we look at the cross and behold the Christ of perfect love we cannot help but be blessed. Jesus revealed the true nature of the loving Father. His love is not judgmental and punitive but rather merciful and redemptive. The joy of this discovery and the satisfaction of this powerful faith experience is that for which we each must seek and taste and see for ourselves.

Dr. Frederick E. Blumer, in addressing the incoming freshmen class at Lycoming College in Pennsylvania had some sound advice.". . . They (colleges) exist primarily to perform an academic function. But there are always a few who expect them to be more like country clubs than anything else. And, unfortunately, there are even a few faculty and staff who would subordinate scholarship to extra-curricular activities. But I hope most of you came here to learn and that you will keep that objective in the forefront of your minds as you enjoy the rest.

It is amazing how false expectations almost guarantee disappointment and failure. Some come to college expecting it to be like a grocery store, failing to understand that there is no way to sell learning or to merchandise insight. Your teachers aren't salesmen They are midwives, as Socrates observed, who assist in the birth of ideas! So don't expect new knowledge to be dispensed to you like chewing gum from a vending machine. Remember that only you can think your thoughts, and until you think them through, many ideas will remain mysteries to you.

He who seeks will find the truth and the power of God. The open secret will have been discovered. This does not mean that life will always flow along like a song. There will still be hardships, but faith will show you the way.

An inscription in the cellar of Cologne where Jews took refuge in flight from the Nazi terror bears eloquent witness to this. The inscription reads as follows: "I believe in the sun even when it is not shining. I believe in love even when not feeling it. I believe in God even when He is silent."

Dr. Harvey Cox, in his book "The Secular City" reminds us that, once we have made this discovery of God's existence and availability to bless, we will want to share with Him in serving others. He states, "God has chosen man to be his partner." He believes that we should expect great things from man because he is created in the image of God and the creator remains as a partner in love's mission with the created. To love is to live. We love to come alive. We serve to keep living. Jane Adams of Hull House in Chicago spoke of Halstead Street as a "river of men." These men represented the soiled and seamy of life. Miss Adams said, "I soil my hands in the river but it cleanses my soul." What a privilege it is to let others know that "we care." Anyone attending an Alcoholics Anonymous meeting will see these words. Those who have been helped are eager to help others. They will not hesitate to become involved. There is a world of people who are hurting and need to know that somebody cares.

Henry Ward Beecher, one cold, rainy day came across a little newsboy on the streets of Brooklyn. The lad's papers were soaked by the rain and torn by the wind. He was standing there crying. Picking the boy up in his arms the great man asked, "What is the matter, my little man?" A smile broke across the rain-streaked face and the boy said, "Nothing is the matter now that you've come."

If we want to learn to know more about God we read his word, the Bible, carefully and prayerfully. We will take a serious look at the life of Christ and try to live His way. We will go further to minister to the hurts of others in His name. In so doing our faith will grow and we will be blessed with the discovery of what life is all about.

Hungers of the Human Heart

Chapter 6
Power for Your Life
You shall receive power when the Holy Spirit has come upon you. -Acts 1:8

You, too can live the quality of life for which you inwardly yearn. There is a power available to you. The source and the force for living is God. The Christian believes it is the God revealed in Jesus. He lived as no man has lived. He loved and served more completely than any person in all history. He was crucified, dead and buried. He arose. He lives! His spirit is set loose in the world to bless. To be aware of Him as a living reality is to receive power adequate for living life as it was meant to be lived.

We are told that the followers of Jesus, His disciples, "were filled with joy and the Holy Spirit".(Acts 13:52.) This evaluation of their experience followed their awareness of His return as a living spirit whose presence brought this joy. Each one of us can discover a direction for our life if we become aware of this living spirit. We will become convicted of our sin, both for the things we do that we ought not to do as well as for the much good we ought to do but just don't seem to get accomplished. When we repent and are heartily sorry we become freed of any unnecessary guilt. To really repent is to receive the gift of forgiveness. The love of Christ frees us. It also unites us with others. When we gain this freedom we are more ready to understand the words of St. Augustine when he said, "Love God and do what you please." There was a time in his life when he was burdened with a form of slavery due to his own sinfulness. When he changed, or shall we say, when he allowed God to change him, he became a new man. His words "Love God and do what you please," do not mean for one minute "that anything goes." It means that when we really do love God we will want to do only that which pleases Him. We will not prostitute self, nor use or abuse any other person. We will desire only what is best for all of God's children.

Deep down inside each of us there is a hunger to receive this kind of freedom and this power for life.

The main thing is to let it happen. So many of us, so much of the time, work too hard at it. The word "let" is significant. We do not have to pull or push a stream. We can flow with it. It cuts its own channel and cleans as it flows. Jesus referred to himself as "the living water." You and I desire to flow with love's stream. Gene Bartlett has said, "We only thirst for that which we have tasted." Less struggling and striving, anxious worry and fretting and more loving and letting will do the job.

For too long we have overemphasized the telling of stories about the Jesus of history to the neglect of the Christ of faith. We have lectured, preached, and exhorted about systems of ethics and morality to the neglect of patient waiting before God until we could receive the power by which we could live the good life. Our accent has been on our work and our doing. It is easier to do something than to be somebody. It is true "Faith without works is dead." Modern man needs also to know that works without faith is dead! In the early sixties, following the so-called religious revival of the fifties, some of us were saying that our overcrowded schedules within the church might well be keeping us from facing our real spiritually impoverished selves. Our large budgets, our large and growing buildings filled with bustling activity could well be the beginning flush of a fatal fever instead of a sign of spiritual health and vitality.

The church has buildings but little boldness.

The church has numbers but little nerve.
The church has comfort but little courage.
The church has status but little spirit.
The church has prestige but little power.

We need spirit and power! From where does it come? It comes from God. We need to be aware of the eternal fact that God is alive and at work in his world today. His Holy Spirit can enter our lives and transform ordinary activity into redemptive deeds of love.

The Beatitudes, by and large, deal with qualities of being, not doing. "Blessed are the pure in heart." Not blessed is the man who gives a big pledge to his church. That's a lot easier than to be pure in heart. It is even easier to keep that pledge paid up than it is to be pure in heart. But Jesus said, "Blessed are the pure in heart." This is a quality of being. "Blessed are the poor in spirit." Can't we see it! The Master, knowing the need of people like ourselves, stressed the qualities of being from which doing is a logical result but without which all of our doing will be to no real and lasting good.

I am willing to take my share of blame for our lack of power within our lives. Some time ago I was asked to bring the keynote message at the annual meeting of a church gathering. They assigned me the topic "The Dynamic Word Through the Holy Spirit." The emphasis had to be on the Holy Spirit. Like any minister I went to my files to refer to that which I had read and filed in previous years. I made an amazing discovery! Spiritually it hit me right between the eyes! I didn't have much of a file on the Holy Spirit. I had a big, thick file on the promotion of church attendance. Can't get people to church unless you promote, you know. And you ought to see my files on church finance! You can't run a church without money. There are several big, thick files on stewardship and finance, and it's good material. I have files on the ecumenical spirit and movement as evidenced locally, nationally, and worldwide in the Council of Churches. It is of utmost importance that we participate in the blending of our efforts together with one another in council work — to do together what no group can do alone. I have thick files on this. But when I looked for the Holy Spirit I found a very thin file.

That said something to me! It too, have been active. I've been promoting. I've been a pusher and a plugger. Perhaps you've been the same. How thick is your file on the Holy Spirit? How many references have you clipped on the work of the Holy Spirit? We who are active, we who are doing, we who have so little faith, and we who trust the Holy Spirit so little that it makes you wonder whether we are aware there is such a thing as a God who is alive and at work in his world! There will never, no never, be life-giving power unless we trust the power of God. He is alive and at work in his world and in our lives. As we become increasingly aware of his loving presence we are healthier and happier.

The British Medical Journal reminds us that "There is not a tissue in the human body wholly removed from the influence of the spirit." We are increasingly learning that there is a very close relationship between our emotions, what we think, and the state of our physical body as well as our spiritual health. If we get our spiritual life, our mental attitude, and our emotions adequately cared for we become healthier and happier.

Show me a person or a church who believes God is alive and at work in this world and I will show you a person or a church with health, joy and power. This does not mean we will be relieved from loneliness, hurt and sorrow. It does mean we will have power to cope with life whatever comes. We will understand the beautiful truth of the words of Thomas Moore, "Earth has no sorrow that heaven cannot heal."

The most difficult hurts of life deal not so much with the flesh as with the inner life. When we feel rejected and lonely there is an agony beyond words to describe. It needs to be pointed out, however, that just as the worst hurts are deep inside, so is the greatest strength. God meets us in the deep within, to strengthen us and to aid us in our quest for a new life and a hope that will never disappoint. We do not need to continue to walk in the darkness of despair. There are no hopeless cases. There is a power in our communication with the Divine that overcomes our loneliness, that heals our hurts, and prepares us for a continuing meaningful relationship with other people. In fact, many times we are more understanding of others, as well as ourselves, after we have worked through heartache and discovered this power.

You may remember what Louisa May Alcott says of the deformed Dick Brown in "Little Men." His affliction was a crooked back. He bore his burden so cheerfully that Demi once asked him in his queer way, 'Do humps make people good-natured? I'd like one for myself if they do." We know it never happens automatically. And yet many of us know what Paul was speaking of (he too had a thorn in his flesh) when he said, "We know that in everything God works for good with those who love Him." (Romans 8:28.) A loving person, open to the indwelling of God's presence will find, in time, that even the negatives work for positive good. The secret is to keep loving. To love is to trust. As we love we find it easier to be meaningfully related to other people. In fact, we hunger for a companionship with depth.

There was a little fellow who asked his mother where she was born. She said she was born in Illinois. Then he turned to his dad and inquired, "Daddy, where were you born?" Daddy replied, "I was born in Indiana." And then he asked, "Where was I born?" His daddy said, "You were born in Arizona." To this the lad exclaimed, "My isn't it nice we could all get together?" It is more than nice, it is absolutely necessary that we who seek power in our lives relate to one another in love and honesty. Regular worship in the church of our choice will aid in the discovery of a spiritual power for living life freely and fully.

In the second chapter of Acts when it refers to the day of Pentecost, it reminds us that Pentecost came to a people who were gathered together in one place. Even plain simple geography has something to say about power in the church. Just the coming together in the same place for the same purpose will help give power. It didn't come to these people when they were alone. It came to them when they were together in one place; tarrying until they were endued with power from on high even as he had promised they would he. As you read through the Acts you find that the church was a mighty instrument, a powerful instrument, not because of its own strength, but because of the power that came from the presence of God's Holy Spirit.

The nineteenth chapter of Acts tells of Paul's visit to Ephesus There he found a group of disciples. They were eagerly awaiting Paul's word of advice to them. They had been converted. These were the Christians who had accepted Christ. And so Paul, while he was there, asked them this question, "Did you receive the Holy Spirit when you believed?" And they said, "No, we have never even heard that there is a Holy Spirit" Even the church is full of people who don't know the joy of the living presence. This is why we have so little power individually. This is why the church has so little power collectively. We don't even know there is such a thing as the Holy Spirit. Power and joy are spiritual twins. They come together. They are gifts of his Holy Spirit.

We sing,

> Holy, Holy, Holy! Lord God Almighty!
> God in Three Persons, (Father, Son, and Holy Spirit)
> blessed Trinity.

We fail at times to understand what this means, if we believe it at all. How can God be three persons? I know that it's easy to oversimplify, but let us make a simple analogy. Here's a man. To his mother he is a son, to his wife he is a husband, to his children he is a father. He's all three in one. He's the same person, but he's three in one in different relationship to different people. In somewhat the same manner, but of course in a more sublime and serious way, God is three in one. He is Father, he is Son, he is Holy Spirit — a blessed Trinity. And we cannot possibly know God as Father and appreciate and appropriate the gift of his Holy Spirit unless we receive him. "You shall receive power," the scriptures say, "when the Holy Spirit has come upon you " (Acts 1:8.) He didn't say you would receive power when you take a basket of groceries to a needy family twice a year — Thanksgiving and Christmas. "You shall receive power when the Holy Spirit has come upon you."

Within the last few decades we have witnessed one of the most significant happenings that has ever occurred in the realm of the scientific world, namely the release of atomic energy. We have found the key to that which can unlock the seething, invisible, electrical forces that are inherent in matter. The very piece of furniture upon which you now are seated as you read is not static; it looks solid; it appears that nothing is moving, but it is. These electrical forces in matter have been here; we just recently discovered them. And now man has learned so much that he knows how to split the atom and unleash power, the like of which we never dreamed was humanly possible. In a more wonderful way, just as atomic energy represents the release of hidden forces in the physical world, so Pentecost represents the release of hidden and invisible forces in the realm of personality. God, we believe, can release such power through individuals that it can make atomic power look like a kindergarten boy's plaything. If we believe that God is Almighty, if we believe his son, the Christ is a living reality in our midst, then we can be blessed beyond our ability to describe.

The great scientist, Dr. Charles Steinmetz has helped us to realize the power within. He indicated that he believed, "Some day we shall take God and prayer into the laboratory, and when we do, we shall accomplish more in one generation that we have in the last fifty." Many of us believe that we are on the verge of a great spiritual awakening. There is a new wind blowing.

The other side of the coin, to which we must call attention, is that it is so easy to miss this "new wind" and breath of the spirit. A number of the close followers of Jesus, who should have known better, missed it for a while. It was after the resurrection that Christ appeared and walked with several of them for a number of miles, but they didn't know who it was. He exclaimed, "O foolish men, and slow of heart to believe all that the prophets have spoken!" (Luke 24:25.) After he spent some time with them they acknowledged that their eyes were opened and that they recognized him adding, "Did not our hearts burn within us while he talked to us on the road, while he opened to us the scriptures?' (Luke 24:32.) They surely understood more completely what Jeremiah had declared years before when he said, "There is in my heart as it were a burning fire." (Jer. 20:9.) When we are aware of the living Lord as a loving companion who journeys with us down the highway of life we do have hearts that are warmed with a new joy and assurance. The old hymn, "In the Garden" says, "And he walks with me and he talks with me and tells me I am his own." Talk about the security of love, this is it! It is available to all.

This author is thankful for the church which he loves. It is from her ministry that I have learned the joy of what I am sharing with you. And yet I feel that today so many of our institutional churches are more concerned with maintenance than with mission. We spend so much time in meetings that we have little time for meeting one another and God in any depth relationship. At times we are so active in self seeking and so critical of those who do not believe as we do, it is utterly amazing what damage is done in the name of religion! How desperately we need to be guided by God's loving Spirit! Unless the spirit of compassion, so perfectly made known in Christ, motivates us, we can readily be used of the evil one, whether we be in or out of the church.

The late Alben Barkley had a story of a church that wouldn't pay its contractor. He sent them bill after bill and they never replied. When they had a revival he went to the service but not as a worshiper. He dressed up to look like the devil — red suit, horns, tail, and all. Toward the close of the service he appeared at the window of the church and jumped right down in front of the sanctuary. Well, without announcement, they left. The preacher left; the choir left; the congregation left just as fast as they could. They all were gone — amazing what people do when the devil comes to church! They all got out but one poor old lady. She stumbled and fell up front. She couldn't get up. The devil came and leaned over her and leered at her. She said, "Don't you bother me!" She added, "I have been a member of this church for sixty-one years. I sang in the choir for many, many years. I've taught in the Sunday school God only knows how long. I have been on the official board for forty years," and she added, "I have baked hundreds, if not thousands of pies for church suppers." And then she said, "But I have been on your side all along." It could well be unless we're careful, those of us in the church without thinking through, without praying through, without loving through, might be instruments of the devil. Oh, how we need to be directed by the Holy Spirit!

The Holy Spirit is more than a doctrine. It is an experience. Those filled with his power know the joy of Immanuel — "God with us." We need to experience this Divine Companionship. Christ has said, "Lo, I am with you always." (Matt. 28:20.) We either know this for a fact or we don't. John Wesley once said, "I am not afraid that the people called Methodists should ever cease to exist . . . but I am afraid lest they should exist only as a dead sect, having the form of religion without the power." This can well be the wholesome concern of every one of us regardless of our denominational affiliation.

Why was Wesley's great day so long in coming?
He always felt that the fault was not altogether his own.
He groped in the dark for many years and nobody helped
him - - not even his ministers. William Law was one
of those ministers, and Wesley afterwards wrote him
on the subject, 'How will you answer to our common
Lord,' he asks, 'that you, sir, never led me into the light?
Why did I scarcely ever hear you name the name of
Christ? Why did you never urge me to faith in his blood?
Is not Christ the First and Last? If you say that you
thought I had faith already, verily, you know nothing
of me. I beseech you sir, by the mercies of God,
to consider whether the true reason of your never
pressing this salvation upon me was not this — that you
never had it yourself!'

Hungers of the Human Heart

Here is a letter for a man like Wesley to write to a man like Law! Many a minister has since read that letter on his knees and has prayed that he may never deserve to receive so terrible a reprimand.[1]

It happened to Wesley in a meeting on Aldersgate Street in London, May 24, 1738. This was the turning point of his life. It was his spiritual watershed. Before he knew about God's love in Christ. Now he knew him personally. His was an experienced religion. He knew his sins were forgiven and the reality of the Presence. Thus his "heart was strangely warmed."

Many have gone into a hospital sickroom and there seen a person so weak he couldn't even lift a hand off the bed. The body, particularly the face would be pale, a sickening pale color. Later you have seen that person after they've been given a blood transfusion. Now the person's face is rosy, and there is a newness of life. He can lift his hand off the bed to greet you. There's a sign of vitality because he's had a transfusion of life-giving blood. Our lives so lacking in spirit, in boldness, and in power today need a life-giving transfusion of God's Holy Spirit. This can never be man induced or directed. It is the gift of God, sent from him to those who will receive it.

William Stiger tells of a master artist who could produce beautiful windows. He had a studio in Boston. His students marveled. One time he had a dinner meeting and Bill Stiger happened to be there. He said the artist related an experience. "We thought he was telling it on himself, though he did not mention himself." He told of a young boy who was studying under the master. The boy couldn't produce the same kind of beautiful stained glass windows as his master-artist teacher. And so he said to the teacher, "Can't I please use your tools? I'd like to see if I can do the work you do." The master loaned him the tools. Several weeks later he checked back to see how the boy was doing. The boy said, "I'm not doing any better than I was with my tools. I'm not making any headway." That

[1] F. W. Boreham, A Bunch of Everlastings (New York: The Abingdon Press, 1920). Used by permission of The Epworth Press. Pp. 208-9.

80

particular day there happened to be another great master artist visiting the studio. He looked at the boy and said, "Son, it isn't the tools of the master you need. It's the spirit of the master you need." Is this not true for you and me?

Although we will never agree on doctrine we can agree to love God and one another as He first loved us through his son. Some years ago, when I had first written this book (before this revised edition) Dr. Albert Schweitzer wrote me a letter of appreciation for its contents. In it he said "... am glad in your will to live in the spirit of the Lord Jesus." I have heard fellow Christians argue heatedly about Dr. Schweitzer's Christology. After having spent a week in his African village hospital, working with him, eating with him, talking and worshiping with him, and after seeing the fruit of his labor, I must say that he possessed and was possessed by the true spirit of the Master Physician in whose name he served and healed.

Once, when he was in America, in New York City, he walked past a newsstand a number of times. A friend of mine later was visiting with the news man. He referred to the distinguished visitor. "Is that the foreign-looking man with the droopy mustache?" My friend replied, "Yes." He then added, "He must be a great, great man. Just as he walks past me he makes me wonder at a sort of inside bigness." This is it! Inside bigness is our business.

In his book, *The Imitation of Christ*, Douglas V. Steere says, "Since you are not an angel but a man, you will run down daily and like a clock you must be rewound." His whole book stresses the importance of a daily habit of opening ourselves for renewal. The heart hungers of your life and mine are more apt to be fulfilled if we will read the Bible, meditate on its contents, and commune daily with God. We call this prayer. No one of us should ever neglect the development of the inner life. This is the source of our power. It is also the source of health. It is from the Anglo-Saxon "halig" we find our word "holy", it is like "hal", which means "whole" or "well". "Spirit" means "the breath of life." To be open, receptive, and responsive to God within is to avail ourselves of a wealth and a wholeness of life for which we were intended. But let's not try too hard at this. Let us trust.

Dr. Wayne E. Oates, Professor of Psychiatry and Behavioral Sciences, University of Louisville School of Medicine, and Doctor of Clinical Pastoral Education, reminds his patients that most of us try too hard. We are afraid that we might fail and that God, whom we perceive as a tyrant will destroy us. Dr. Oates reminds us that Jesus, who was very aware of the anxious efforts of fearful people, turned and spoke of the lilies of the field. They grow serenely, without strain, overexertion, and fretful worries about approval. The sun and the rain bless them and they grow at the pace for which they were created. As a helper of many people, Dr. Oates says, "Trying too hard is one source of anxiety. When we begin to think God's love for us is determined by our efforts we are on our way to a sick religion. Our faith becomes healthy when we know it is God who works in us to do His own good pleasure. We rely by faith in the grace of God to energize us from within by his spirit, not upon a fretful and feverish effort to prove ourselves acceptable to God who has already accepted us."[2] We are healthy when we know we are loved and accepted. We then can reach out with love and acceptance to each other. We can also find strength for living each day by developing the inner life. The power comes from within. It is the power of God to those who believe.

Each of us can well pray, even as we sing Edwin Hatch's significant words:

> Breathe on me, Breath of God,
> Fill me with life anew,
> That I may love what Thou dost love,
> And do what Thou wouldst do.
>
> Breathe on me, Breath of God,
> Until my heart is pure,
> Until with Thee I will one will,
> To do and to endure.

[2]The Upper Room Disciplines 1976. Nashville, Tennesee. Used by permission. p. 315.

Breathe on me, Breath of God,
Till I am wholly Thine,
Till all this earthly part of me
Glows with Thy fire divine.

Breathe on me, Breath of God,
So shall I never die,
But live with Thee the perfect life
Of Thine eternity.